THIS LAND IS
OUR LAND

THIS LAND IS OUR LAND
The Mohawk Revolt At Oka

Craig MacLaine
Michael S. Baxendale

Photography:
Robert Galbraith

Optimum Publishing International Inc.
Montréal - Toronto 1990

This Land is Our Land: The Mohawk Revolt at Oka
Copyright © 1991, Optimum Publishing International Inc.

Legal deposit 4th quarter 1990
National Library of Canada
Legal deposit 3ieme trimester 1990
Bibliotheque National du Québec.

Canadian Cataloguing in Publication Data

MacLaine, Craig, 1955-

    This land is our land: the Mohawk revolt at Oka

ISBN 0-88890-230-1 (bound).—
    ISBN 0-88890-229-8 (pbk.)

    1. Quebec (Province)—History—Native
Crisis, 1990.   2. Mohawk Indians—History.
3. Iroquois Indians—Constitutional law.
4. Indians of North America—Quebec
(Province)—History.   5. Indians of North
America—Constitutional law.   1. Baxendale,
Michael S., 1937–   11. Galbraith, Robert,
1956–   111. Title.

E99.M8M33 1990   971.4'04   C90-090567-0

For information, address:
Optimum Publishing International Inc.,
4255 Ste. Catherine St. West,
Montréal, Qc.
H3Z lP7

News Text: *Craig MacLaine*

Historical Sketches: *Michael S. Baxendale*

Photography: *Robert Galbraith*

Editor: *Laurel Sulivan*

Maps: *Reda Kaddour*

Editor in Chief: *Michael S. Baxendale*

Typestyles: Body type, Times Roman
                          Headings, Optima
                          Set by: LitoPresse Inc., Montreal

Printed and Bound in Canada
on acid free, environmentally friendly paper

Acknowledgements

The Authors wish to thank all who were so helpful to us throughout this project. We must especially name: John Cree, Ellen Gabriel, Margaret Gabriel, Debbie Etienne, Mavis Etienne, Marie David, and Beverley Nelson of Kanesatake; Dale Diome, Louis Hall, Johnny Beauvais, Danny Kanistanaron of Kahnawake; Ian Barrett of Reuters, Major John Paul Macdonald of the Canadian Army, Niall Russell of Diamond Books and all the people of the Mohawk Nation.

Contents

Introduction   This is a book about a tiny band of Indians who said "Enough." Enough to a
people they had welcomed to their land four and a half centuries ago but who now
wanted to rob them of their last heritage and take it for themselves. It is also the
story of the lethargy of governments and fatal miscalculations made by a
provincial police force. At the same time it is the story of a well-disciplined army
that did the job it was sent to do. There were no clear cut victors in this war but
the Mohawk Iroquois gave notice that they meant it when they said: "Enough!"

We have written *This Land is our Land* as it happened, and from where it
happened. Collectively we spent some 150 days and/or nights at Kanesatake and
Kahnawake. We started to write the book the week Corporal Lemay died. The
manuscript was completed just one month after the Mohawk Warriors walked out
of the Treatment Center at Oka on September 26. Time has not yet tempered the
raw events of the Summer of 1990. The bitter confrontations and scenes of
violence are fresh in our minds.

The chronological narrative covers the hard news events beginning in March
of 1990 when the Kanesatake Mohawks set up their barricade on a sandy track
near the golf course at the town of Oka, Québec. We have avoided introspective
observations, except as eye witness interpretations of the actual events. The
historical sketches are based on dozens of interviews with the Mohawk and
reference to scores of documents and historical records. We felt them necessary
to bring this event into historical perspective. The photography was chosen from
more than 4,000 frames taken between March 11 and September 26 when the last
of the Warriors laid down their arms. In fact, photojournalist Galbraith lived the
last seventeen days of the crisis within the TC compound with the holdout
Warriors. For a better understanding of the Six Nation Iroquois Confederacy of
which the Mohawk people are a part we have published *The Great Law of Peace*
in its entirety, perhaps for the first time in a non-native publication.

What struck us more and more as we watched events unfold and pursued the
background to them was that the events at Oka were not new. Unfortunately it is
a story repeated down through our history and it is not a proud one for Canadians.
Only history will tell if we have learned from the events of the summer of 1990.

We wanted to provide as complete and accurate a record as possible of what
happened, this time.

I hope we have accomplished this.

M. S. B.
Editor-in-Chief
Montréal, October 1990

This land is ours; ours by right of possession;
ours as a heritage,
given to us as a sacred legacy.
It is the spot where our fathers lie;
beneath those trees our mothers sang our lullaby,
and you would tear it from us
and leave us wanderers at the mercy of fate.

Joseph Onasakenarat,
Chief of the Oka Mohawk, 1868

THE CRISIS

March 11 to September 26, 1990

Sunday, March 11, 1990　　The Mohawk of the Kanesatake settlement had run out of legal options. The courts had rejected their attempts to block development of the Pines, a small forest bordering the Québec resort town of Oka. For the Mohawk, the Pines is a special place. It is there that the Mohawk of Kanesatake gather with their friends and family to reaffirm their commitment to each other, to the land, and to the Mohawk way of life. It is there, as well, that they bury their dead.

*Oka from
the Ottawa
River*

But the Oka town council had other ideas for the land. As a resort town, Oka needed something to attract more visitors from nearby Montréal. An 18-hole golf course would do the trick. A 9-hole course already existed.

All that was needed would be to expand the course onto the Mohawk-claimed land. And the courts had agreed that the land belonged to the whites, not the Indians.

The Kanesatake Mohawk decided they would not stand by and watch what they believed was another case of the white man stealing Indian land. And on this day, they erected their first blockade across a dirt road leading into the Pines. Mohawk men armed with rifles took up positions at the barricade. They issued a warning to the Oka town council. No one would be permitted to enter the Pines, they said. We are prepared to fight...and if necessary, to die...in defense of our land.

The would-be developers of the golf course took the threat seriously. No work crews would be sent in as long as the Mohawk remained at the barricade.

A long, drawnout but peaceful standoff had begun with the men of the Kanesatake band taking turns keeping watch at the barricade. There was nothing to guard against...for now. Oka town council would be doing its work in the courts.

Saturday, June 30, 1990

After three-and-a-half months of legal work, the Oka town council succeeded in winning a court order to have the roadblock removed. The Québec Superior Court ruled that the Mohawk were illegally preventing development of the land and must halt all efforts aimed at keeping the work-crews off the disputed land.

The Mohawk had no intention of obeying the court order. But the action did serve as a warning that the white authorities were running out of patience and would not allow things to continue as they were for much longer.

War, feared the Mohawk, was coming.

Tuesday, July 10, 1990

The Mohawk were almost certain that an attack would be made within days. Earlier in the week, Québec's minister for Native Affairs John Ciaccia had sent a plea to Oka mayor Jean Ouellette: Don't force the issue. Put the golf course expansion at least on hold while we try to come up with some kind of peaceful solution to the dispute.

Mayor Ouellette ignored the plea. He said the law is the law, the courts have ruled, and now it is the duty of the police to uphold the rulings. He called for the Sûreté du Québec, the provincial police force, to be sent in without delay.

The Mohawk spent the day reinforcing their defenses. They strung up barbed wire through the trees. Logs, barrels and sandbags were used to build bunkers from which the Mohawk could fire on their attackers. Some of the defenders were members of the paramilitary Warrior Society whose role it is under the 1,000-year-old Mohawk constitution to defend Mohawk territory. The Warriors were armed with assault rifles. Some of the Warriors had served as volunteers in the United States armed forces. A few had seen action in Vietnam. The Warriors knew how to defend a position and how to prevent an attacker from outflanking them.

Mayor Ouellette of Oka

The first barricade

Wednesday, July 11, 1990

Highway 344 runs east-west through the southern tip of the Pines. From the town of Oka running west, the two-lane highway climbs a steep hill. Just before the top, the golf course clubhouse can be seen on the right-hand or northern side.

Looking south, there is a spectacular view of the Lake of Two Mountains and the Ottawa River.

Just as the road begins to level out, there is the Mohawk cemetery on the northern side. It is a small, well-kept Christian cemetery. Several generations of Kanesatake Mohawk are buried there. On Sundays, Mohawk with rakes and clippers come to groom their family grave sites.

The Mohawk cemetery at Oka

On the western side of the cemetery runs the narrow access road that links the highway to the golf club parking lot. The road curves around the cemetery cutting it off from the rest of the Pines. Past the golf course road is the sacred pine tree forest which stretches westward for a kilometer. The main access road into the Pines leads north off the highway some 300 meters past the golf course road. The Pines road dips down a meter-and-a-half from the highway. It then levels out and curves first right and then left back into the forest. In front of the first curve, the Mohawk have built a lacrosse box. It looks like an ice hockey rink. There are goal nets and wire meshing above the boards at each end of the field.

On the highway side – the south side – of the box is a large open space for spectators. It is in this area the Mohawk children play while the parents talk and spread out their picnics. And on this day, it was here where the Mohawk women and children were camping out in defense of their land.

On the northern side, the brush and the forest has crept up almost to the boards. Protected by the cover of the forest, the Mohawk men who were armed with rifles had spread out to protect the barricade and their flanks.

The barricade had been built across the entrance to the Pines just a few meters off the highway.

Just before dawn, the first of the Sûreté du Québec police officers began to arrive in cars and rented vans. They parked along the side of the highway and got out. The officers were armed with rifles and tear gas. They wore bullet-proof vests and gas masks.

Some of the Mohawk women and most of the children were still asleep. Others had just risen and were preparing breakfast. They were frying up sausages and eggs for the breakfast. The children would be getting peanut butter and jam sandwiches. Johnny Cree, a spiritual leader for the traditional Longhouse at Kanesatake, was leading a prayer. It was a prayer of thanks to the Creator for sending sunlight to the world for another day. The Mohawk burned tobacco. Its smoke, according to their tradition, carries their prayers up to the Creator.

Once the SQ officers had assembled, they moved toward the barricade. One of the officers told the women to bring forward their spokesman.

"You are talking to our spokesmen," answered one of the women. "You're talking to our women and children. There are children here. Don't point your guns at us."

The officer ignored the woman and again asked to speak to a Mohawk spokesman. But the women had been telling the truth. The Mohawk rule their communities by consensus and the women have a strong role in developing that consensus.

When the women at the barricade failed to bring up anyone to act as a spokesman, the SQ fired a couple of tear gas cannisters which exploded with a loud bang. That woke the women who were still sleeping. They woke up in time to see the cloud of gas rolling toward them. Unable to see, the gas stinging their eyes and burning their throats, the women retreated to a point 100 meters to the north-east of the barricade. More tear gas was fired. Some of the women held their breath, squinted their eyes, and made their way through the smoke back up to the front to plead with the police.

"We've got our children here," they said. "You're hurting our kids."

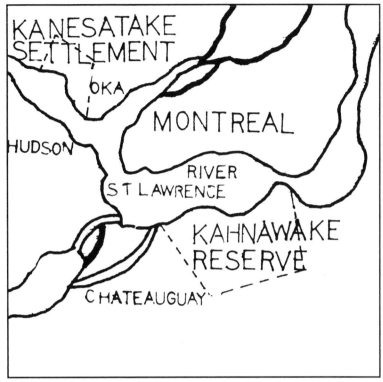

Montréal area indicating location of Kanesatake and Kahnawake

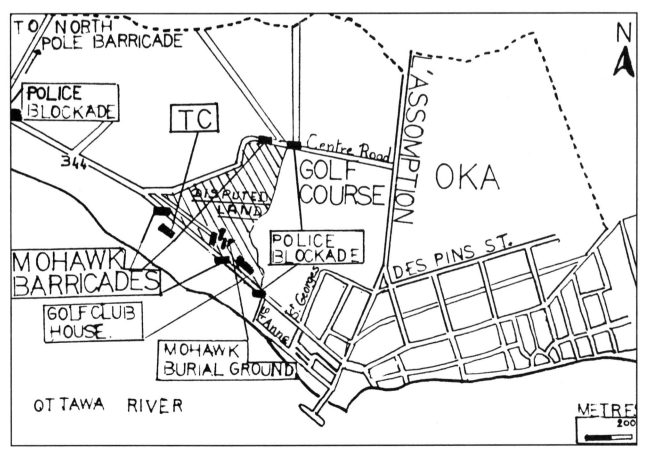

Mohawk and police barricades around town of Oka

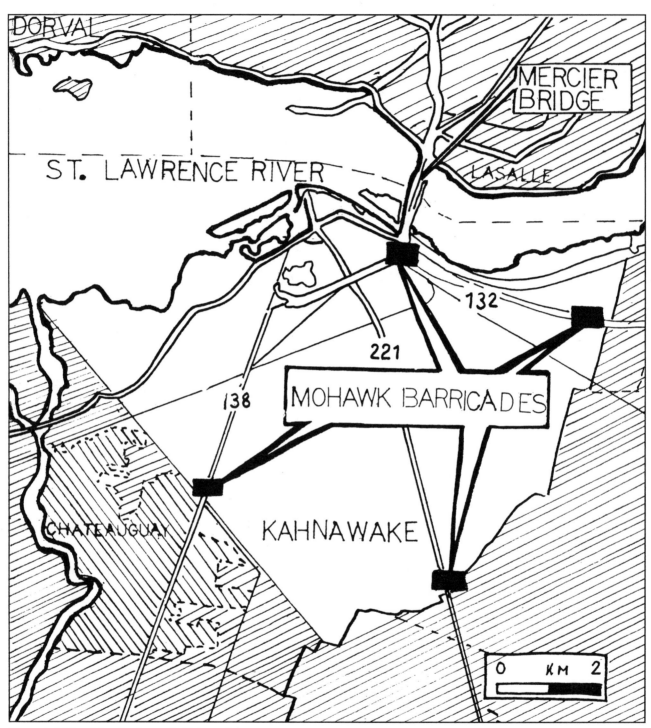

The main Mohawk barricades on the Kahnawake reserve

The Barricade on Highway 344, Oka

The Barricade on the Mercier Bri

Press conference at Kahnawake, 1 to r.:
Chief Billy Two Rivers, legal council Owen Young, negotiators
Mavis Etienne and Andrew Delisle

Riot police in Chateaugu

The SQ officer in charge repeated his demand to meet with a Mohawk spokesman.

The women asked Johnny Cree to come up and speak to the police. He agreed.

The smoke from the tear gas was dispersing and Cree walked up to the barricade.

"Are you the leader?" asked the SQ officer.

"No, I'm just a spokesperson," said Cree. "There is no leader. The people lead."

The officer was used to dealing under a disciplined command structure. It was frustrating for him to attempt to negotiate with a group where no one and everyone is a leader. Nevertheless, he continued with his efforts.

Do you understand that we have orders to enforce a court injunction against this barricade? he asked. We are obliged to dismantle the barrier with or without your consent.

Cree answered that the Pines is a sacred place for the Mohawk. It's like a church. Besides, he said, there are women and children here defending their land. You can't attack them.

The officer said he understood all that but it was out of his hands. He was a policeman following orders, he had a job to do, and he was going to do it.

Cree said he would talk to the people. He would tell them what the police had told him, and he would ask if they had changed their minds. He also asked for time to finish the religious ceremony that had been interrupted by the first volley of tear gas. The officer said he would give the Mohawk five minutes. After that, the police would move in. Cree said he needed an-hour-and-a-half. Out of the question, said the officer. But he said he was willing to compromise. The Mohawk would have 45 minutes.

Cree went back to the clearing near the lacrosse box and finished the dawn ceremony. Then he talked with the women and the few men that were not deployed back in the bush.

By this time, more police had arrived. Cars and vans were lining both sides of the Highway. The elite assault team of the Sûreté du Québec was there. Its members were dressed in dark green combat uniforms and helmets. They wore gas masks. Bullet-proof vests known as flak jackets added to their bulk. They carried assault rifles. Overhead, an SQ helicopter hovered attempting to spot the Mohawk men in the brush. The police were not certain of what kind of an armed force they were facing. All they could see were women, children, and a few men armed only with baseball bats.

The police plan was to put on a display of overwhelming force in the hope that the Mohawk would see the futility of fighting and would surrender the barricade without any violence.

Cree told the people that it looked as if the police were serious. He said they had guns and combat gear and it looked as if they were ready to do more than simply arrest anyone who resisted them. He warned them that blood might be shed if they did not back off. And he asked them to consider leaving the area until the danger had passed.

They said no, they were staying. It was their last piece of sacred land. Without it, they would not be able to live as Mohawk at Kanesatake. To abandon it would be to abandon themselves.

"Of course, I'm scared," said one of the women. "But I'm going to stay and fight."

Cree went back to the barricade to tell the SQ officer that the Mohawk would not leave. Again, the SQ officer said he had a job to do and it would be done. He told Cree that for their own safety, the women and children at least should be moved across the highway on to the police side of the line.

Cree said he doubted they would go for it but he would tell them of the offer.

By now, he was frightened that a real battle would break out. He pleaded with the men and women to reconsider. They told him they couldn't. And they asked him to offer up a prayer for their protection. He called on the Creator to protect the Mohawk. Shelter the children, he prayed. Cover their eyes and ears to protect their hearts and minds so that they will not carry hatred with them as a result of this day. And whatever the police choose to throw at us, turn it back at them.

Farther west down Highway 344, some of the Mohawk men were building a barrier of burning tires to prevent other SQ vehicles from arriving. Other Mohawk men brought up cars and pickup trucks to reinforce the main blockade. Two of the men came out of the woods carrying a chain saw. They pulled the cord and the saw whined into action. The men began cutting down a large tree in order to block a side road into the area where the women and children were waiting. Policemen had moved into the woods on the western side of the main barricade. And two of them fired tear gas cannisters in the direction of the Mohawk before fleeing back to the highway.

Ellen Gabriel, who would go on to become the main spokesman for the Kanesatake Mohawk during the early days of the crisis, led a group of women up to the police line. The women burnt sweetgrass. They sprinkled the ash on the police. That spooked some of the SQ men.

One woman shouted, "Why do you want to kill me? Why do you want to kill my children?"

She directed her words at one nervous policeman in particular. Slowly, he began to lower his rifle. His officer barked at him to maintain his readiness stance.

The SQ brought in dogs.

There were more than 100 policemen facing the Mohawk. The Mohawk men ordered the women to move back.

The police were standing on their side of the barricade and in the woods on each side. Included in the SQ caravan was a large, yellow front-end loader or bulldozer. It was to be used to dismantle the barricade.

The bulk of the police force assembled in a rough line and began moving forward. They fired tear gas across the barricade toward the Mohawk. The smoke billowed up blocking the Mohawk view of the barricade. For a moment, the women fell back. Then, through the smoke came the sound of the bulldozer moving toward the barricade. Some of the women began moving forward again.

"What the fuck kind of people are they?" said one women in anger. "Over a goddamn golf course and their fucking greedy lust for money."

Another said as she watched the barricade being torn down, "My feeling is let them do it right now. We can always replace it."

Ellen Gabriel

It was a few minutes before 9:00 a.m.

Through the clouds of tear gas, the police assault team appeared moving toward the women and the children. They fired more tear gas and threw concussion grenades. The women and children screamed.

In the bush, the armed men saw the police advancing on their wives and kids. A warcry went up. The gun battle began. Hundreds of rounds were fired. The bullets were coming from both sides. At the height of the battle, the sound of gunfire became a roar in which single shots could not be distinguished. A two-year-old boy was riding his tricycle on the road near the women when the gunfire erupted around him. A man raced out from the bush, grabbed the boy, and dove with him behind a large pine tree. A woman, caught out in the open, tripped as she turned to flee. Another Warrior ran from his cover and threw himself over her body.

Bullet dug out by ballistics experts

In describing the gunbattle, a Mohawk woman named Debbie would later say that it lasted about five minutes but that it seemed to go on forever. In fact, between the first and last shots only 24 seconds elapsed.

Corporal Marcel Lemay was one of the police officers. The 31-year-old father and husband was moving in through a stand of trees west of the barricade. Thirty meters in from the highway, he was hit. He began to hemorrhage almost immediately. His fellow officers were horrified. The ones nearest him fell to the ground beside Lemay. Farther down the line, the other officers had fallen back in the face of the heavy gunfire which was coming from all directions. Many of the bullets were fired over the heads of the police. But others pounded into the trees at chest height. An ambulance sped up to near where Lemay was lying. A medic checked the fallen officer and attempted to staunch the flow of blood. But there was little he could do. Lemay was dragged quickly inside, and the ambulance sped away to the hospital.

Cpl. Marcel Lemay

The police had seen enough. They fled. The wind had shifted and was blowing the clouds of tear gas back toward the highway. Some of the cars and vans had been locked. There was not time to search for keys. The vehicles were abandoned as the officers, some on foot, some in cars, raced down the hill to the safety of Oka where they would wait for reinforcements.

Louis Hall — A Short History of the Montréal Mohawk

Louis Hall, 72, is a well-known painter and poet and a Kahnawake Mohawk. He converted from Catholicism to the traditional ways of the Longhouse while in his early forties. He has been instrumental in interpreting the Great Law of Peace so that his people can know more of their heritage.

"When (Jacques) Cartier came here in 1535 there was a large settlement of Mohawk at Hochelaga (Indian word meaning mossy place). Cartier himself wrote that there were 'at least 50 longhouses'.

"Cartier's first arrival was in October 1535. The Mohawk welcomed his companions and crew which in total were less than thirty-five. More than a thousand Mohawk men, women and children joined in the friendly greeting. Dancing in joy they brought large quantities of fish and bread which they showered down on the boats.

"The next day the natives took Cartier to visit their village. As he walked the path through the beautiful oak forest he remarked that the place was as beautiful as any forest in all Europe. Soon the forest gave way to fields full of the corn. The village was fortified with a tiered, wooden palisade some fifteen-feet high. Within the perimeter were some fifty sturdy houses and in the midst was an open square where Cartier was introduced to the Great Chief."

This was the day Montréal got its name. At Cartier's re-quest the party was guided by the Mohawk in a climb up the mountain. That day the view that awaited Cartier was breathtaking. 'I could see for thirty leagues around,' he said. And he felt the site was worthy of the name 'Royal'. Thus, Mont Royal became the mountain's European name and later the name of the city that grew at its foot.

The day had been so exhausting for some of Cartier's men that the Mohawks' hospitality extended even to picking up the weary and carrying them back to their boats.

"Some seventy years later, (Samuel de) Champlain was out to satisfy the merchants' greed. To solidify France's hold on the fur trade he persuaded the Huron and the Algonquin to side with him against the Iroquois. The Five Nation tribes were consid-ered the most intelligent, best organized, and their warriors the best fighters. But against firearms there was little doubt of the outcome. On Lake Champlain a battle was fought."

(American historian Frances Parkman later described the battle: It was agreed on both sides that the fight would be deferred till daytime; but meantime a commerce of abuse, sarcasm, menace and boasting gave unceasing exercise to the lungs – much says Champlain like besiegers and besieged in a beleagured town.)

"Some of the Mohawk were chased down and killed, others were made prisoner. These prisoners were taken back to the fort at Ville Marie to be used as serfs in the European manner. They were put to work digging and moving stone to build the church and settlement around Place D'Armes. It was Indian labour that built the European settlement at Hochelaga. History has shown that Champlain's decision to make an enemy of the Iroquois proved very costly for the settlers of New France and the mother country.

"For most of the seventeenth century there was war between the Iroquois and the French. The Iroquois raided the French settlements and harassed the river traffic carrying furs to Québec. It was in 1666 that the Sulpicians were confirmed as the Seigneurs of Montréal Island by proclamation of the King of France. That year a huge force of French regulars supported by Canadians and Indian mercenaries invaded Iroquois territory around Lake Champlain and Lake George. The Mohawk scouts alerted the people to the invasion and the villages were empty when the enemy under de Courcelle arrived. The army numbered some thirteen hundred and they burned and pillaged the villages destroying all stocks of food. This 'defeat' so devastated the Indians it brought an uneasy peace to the St. Lawrence Valley for twenty years. Then in the 1680s, as the Iroquois regained some strength, more sorties against the Iroquois were made by La Barre, Denonville, and Frontenac.

"Donnenville thought by capturing and imprisoning the chiefs he would stop Iroquois resistance. He didn't realize the Iroquois always had at least one apprentice understudying for a chief's role ever ready to take his place. In 1687 he gathered a force of some three thousand to teach the Iroquois a lesson. In fact he planned to destroy all Iroquois villages. His militia captain, de Callière, entrapped some friendly Seneca after inviting them to a feast. These were ordered to France to work in the galleys of Louis XIV. Donnenville's force continued into Iroquois territory burning and destroying homes, crops and livestock. The Iroquois thirsted for revenge.

"During this period the Mohawk in Kahnawake remained in semi-serfdom under the thumb of soldiers and the whim of the church. In 1689 the Grand Council of the Iroquois got together in Onondaga and sent a message to the Kahnawake Mohawk. It said that they were putting a force of Indians together to liberate them from serfdom. The Mohawk had been kept under guard by the soldiers and brainwashed by the priests for so long that they did not want to be liberated to 'paganism' again. So, when the Iroquois arrived in Kahnawake the French had taken the Mohawk into the Fort Ville Marie across the St. Lawrence.

"In frustration some fifteen hundred Iroquois warriors crossed Lake St. Louis and fell on Lachine, a fur trading settlement of about 1100. They killed 200, took 900 captive and burned the village. They took the prisoners to the gates of Fort Ville Marie to exchange for the Mohawk serfs. But those commanding the fort refused to bargain. The Iroquois told them they would burn at the stake the Lachine villagers one by one in front of their eyes if they did not release the Mohawk. But serfs were money-in-the-bank so they refused again. The Iroquois proceeded to make good their promise. Over the two month period that they stayed in the Montréal area, they raided the seigneuries down the St. Lawrence as far as Trois Rivieres and wiped out almost half the population of New France.

"When they returned to their lands in upper New York State they took many young children prisoners with them to be brought up with the Iroquois. These infants were to be taught the Indian ways and thus learn how to live properly. The idea was to return them to the white man after they had grown to maturity. By so doing the Iroquois felt they could educate the newcomers towards a better lifestyle. But it didn't work. The French settlers and their church wanted no part of the Great Law of Peace and the ways of the Longhouse. They rejected their own children who were then taken back by the Iroquois and lived out their lives with them.

"In 1697 Frontenac decided to invade the Iroquois Nation with another great force. But this time the Indians had burned most of their villages before them. He did lay waste some Indian villages and killed and tortured the Iroquois that were left. They (the French) took 280 prisoners and were on their way back to Québec with the infirm Frontenac when the Iroquois ambushed them, freed their people, and put the soldiers to flight.

"That was the last attempt to invade Iroquois territory, 1697. And that is what we mean when we say we are an unconquered nation."

The Mohawk men near the western flank saw what was happening behind the tear gas smoke. They ran out after the police and took control of the abandoned police vehicles. By this time, the wind had shifted and was sending the tear gas and smoke rolling down the hill after the police.

The other Mohawk could not, from their position behind and to the east of the barricade, see what was happening behind the smoke. They knew only that the gunfire had stopped for the moment.

One of the armed men came out to where the women were huddled.

"You. All you girls. In the bush. Now," he shouted.

Stunned by the noise and the ferocity of the gunfire, the women stared at him but didn't move.

"All you girls. In the bush," he screamed at them again. "C'mon. In the bush. Go. In the bush. Go."

This time they moved. They still did not know whether the police were coming after them or not.

When the men, women and children had moved far enough back to be out of the line of fire, they stopped.

"Anybody hit? Anyone hurt?" they asked each other.

"I don't know," said one woman. "I saw an ambulance go by."

Some of the women were crying.

"Why don't they stop it?" said one woman who had collapsed in tears.

"Grab hold of yourself," said another. "Don't start." She slapped the crying woman. "Stop."

"Take it easy 'cause...." said the woman who had been slapped.

"'Cause what?" the other woman cut her off. "Get in the woods."

The sound of chainsaws cutting down trees and the beeping noise of the bulldozer moving in reverse came from the front. And as the smoke dispersed, the Mohawk saw that it was a Warrior who was driving the big machine. They knew then that they had won.

While two police helicopters hovered overhead, the Mohawk cheered. Out on the highway, trees had been felled across the road near the entrance to the cemetery creating a new barrier. The Warriors searched through the abandoned police vehicles and stripped them of weapons, ammunition and communication equipment.

The captured bulldozer was paraded through the Pines to loud cheers from the Mohawk who were coming out of the bush. It was then put to work crushing the abandoned police cars and piling them upon the new barricade. Other Warriors built a barricade eight kilometers to the west on Highway 344 and north of Kanesatake on Ste. Germaine road. The three paved roads into the settlement were now blocked off and under Mohawk control. The police were on the outside.

At the eastern end of Oka, the police set up their own barrier at the bottom of the hill leading up 344 toward the Pines. They stared up the hill at the Mohawk who were taunting them from atop their new barricade. Warriors took turns climbing on top of the overturned police cars from where they would wave their rifles in the air and scream out war cries.

With each passing hour, more members of the police were arriving at Oka. At the same time, Corporal Lemay was dying in a hospital bed.

Cpl. Lemay's kit at battle scene

Front-end loader at work on new barricade.

SQ barricade goes up at Oka

Thirty kilometers to the south-east, the Mohawk of the Kahnawake reserve were furious at the police raid. They feared another attack would be launched at any moment against the smaller and less-organized Mohawk at Oka. In support of the Kanesatake band, the Kahnawake Warrior Society blocked all roads into the reserve. Those roads included two major highways as well as the southern tip of the Mercier Bridge. The bridge is a vital link between the island of Montréal and several heavily-populated suburbs lining the south shore of the

St. Lawrence River. As soon as the blockades went up, huge traffic jams formed on the bridge and on all the approach roads. The Kahnawake Mohawk had a warning: We'll bring down the bridge if there is another police assault on the Kanesatake band.

There was no plan other than to wait and see what the police would do at Oka. The blockade of the Mercier Bridge could come down in a matter of hours, days, or weeks. The Mohawk had yet to decide on any long term strategy. They only knew that they wanted to do something.

"Our people had no choice," said Mohawk author and historian Johnny Beauvais. "The people from Kanesatake come over here. We go over there. Their kids go to our school. They're our brothers and sisters. We couldn't just leave them out there on their own."

The police would take no more chances. They set up barricades of their own along the outside perimeter of the reserve and on the northern side of the bridge. Then they waited.

Barricade on Centre Road

Barricade at Kahnawake

In Québec City, Premier Robert Bourassa met with his minister of Public Security, Sam Elkas. They discussed all the possible options the government had in dealing with the crisis. There could be no sign of weakness or of giving in to the Mohawk, they agreed. But they were also aware that the Mohawk could not be defeated quickly without bloodshed. And so, for the moment little would be done except to seal off Kanesatake and Kahnawake.

Thursday, July 12, 1990

When the sun rose, the Warriors saw hundreds of police officers facing them from behind three main barricades. Two of those barricades were on Highway 344 at the eastern and western entrances to Kanesatake. The third was on Centre Road along the northern perimeter of the disputed land.

The question for the Mohawk was when would the next attack come. After the first assault, the call for help had gone out. Mohawk willing to fight for the Kanesatake band were on their way to Oka. Some had already arrived during the night. Among the arrivals were Warriors from the Akwesasne reserve which straddles the Canada-U.S. frontier near Cornwall.

There were three likely courses the police and the authorities would choose.

One would be to attack as quickly as possible. The longer the police waited, the more Warriors there would be. As well, the physical defenses – the barriers, barbed wire, and trenches – were being strengthened by the Mohawk as quickly as they could.

A second possiblility would be for the authorities to try to negotiate a quick settlement. Since the Québec government was not prepared to make any major concessions, it was not realistic to expect that negotiations could bring about a rapid end to the crisis. However, by sending in representatives to talk with the Mohawk, the government would show that it was interested in a peaceful resolution and was not simply out for blood.

The third option would be to do nothing. That would send a message to the Mohawk. It would tell them that there could be no compromise and that the government, with its much greater resources in terms of manpower and weapons, was prepared to sit tight for as long as it might take to force the Mohawk into submission.

Many Warriors expected Premier Bourassa to choose the first option. Instead, however, the premier elected to go with a combination of the second and third choices.

John Ciaccia, the Québec minister in charge of Native Affairs, was sent to Oka to talk with the Mohawk. The first thing he did was to assure them that there would be no more police attacks. But aside from those assurances and promises that he would consider their demands, Ciaccia had little to offer.

In any case, the Mohawk had lost their faith in Ciaccia. Two days before the raid, the minister had publicly pleaded to the town of Oka not to force a confrontation over the golf course. It was apparently without his knowledge that the raid had been ordered. And the Mohawk believed that for all his good intentions, Ciaccia was powerless to control the police or to negotiate on behalf of the Québec government.

As long as the police are out there, armed and in large numbers, we have to expect that another attack will come, said the Mohawk.

The Mohawk and the Land at Oka.

At one time the Six Nations occupied a vast territory stretching from Vermont to Ohio and Québec to Tennessee with hundreds of towns and villages throughout their country.

Indians do not have the same concept of ownership of the land that white people do. Land is given for need not greed, say the Mohawk. If one Mohawk needs to build a house for his family he is given whatever land he needs.

This is the Mohawk version of the events leading up to the crisis at Oka:

When the white man came to settle he asked if he could use our land to build a cabin for shelter and grow food for sustenance. We saw that he had need and we said yes. We could not conceive that he would neither give it back nor acknowledge us as owners. But that is what he did. He just kept it for himself. He reported back to the old world that there was land for the taking and plenty for everyone. He was encouraged in this practice by his church. It declared itself owners of huge tracts of our land. Their spokesmen said that the King of France, who we had never even met, had given it to them. When the church needed money it sold the land it never owned to parishioners or newcomers to the area who built homes and businesses and eventually golf courses.

That is how it happened in Oka. The whole village was built on Indian land. They used and

enjoyed our forest land, too. We welcomed them. Then they wanted to add an extra nine holes to their private golf course by cutting down the sacred pine forest we planted. It is one of the oldest hand-planted pine forests in North America and our ancient burial grounds are within it. This was too much to swallow and we refused to let our dead be disturbed or to let them use the land for that selfish purpose.

In 1718 a few Mohawk, some Huron and a branch of the Algonquin from the settlement at Sault au-Recollet, were moved to Oka. Sixty-one years earlier, in 1657, the Sulpicians had been made temporary managers of the island of Montréal with a mandate to protect it from the Indians. In 1666 this was confirmed by the King of France. For years the Sulpicians had tried to get grants of land in New France. But they were in competition with the Jesuits who were more powerful in the French Court. Unable to win the grants, they instead asked for lands for an Indian Mission. The King of France agreed to provide a nine-square mile tract of land for the mission. It would later be doubled in size. But the grant came with many restrictions, the main one being that the Sulpicians would only hold the land in trusteeship for the Indians. In 1720 the church insisted that about 200 Mohawk religious dissidents from Kahnawake be removed from their village and sent to live at Oka on the shore of the Lake of Two Mountains. It was the principle of divide and conquer.

The Iroquois were frequent invaders of the settlement and it was the Oka Indians who bore the brunt of the attacks on the community. They became its defenders. But as time went by, more and more Iroquois converted to Christianity and many of them gathered at the settlement. The former enemy had now become the settlement's chief strength.

By this time, the Sulpicians in Montréal had become so wealthy that they surpassed the Jesuits. Among their prized pieces of territory was the land bordering the Lake of Two Mountains on part of which dwelt the Oka Indians. But according to the terms of the original grant, the Indians had a claim on the land that would expire only should they leave it or die out. The Indians loved their home and could not be induced to leave. The Sulpicians hoped to change their minds. Privilege after privilege was taken away from the Indians. Grants they were entitled to were stopped. Tithes for the church were collected with greater vigor at a time when income was stopped. Through the government, the church offered to settle the Indians elsewhere. They were even stopped from cutting wood to repair their homes. They grew poorer and poorer.

Eventually, a Protestant Mission came to the area. And in 1869, the Methodists took up the Indians' cause against Rome. But the Catholic church was powerful in Québec, and in the 1930s the Sulpicians began to sell off land they were supposed to be holding in trusteeship for the Indians. Some land exchanged hands several times although the original sale was not valid, at least as far as the Mohawk were concerned.

And so the fight over who holds title to the land at Kanesatake continues today for the 1600 Mohawk living there.

The preceding is a compilation of interviews with several Mohawk including Danny Karistanoron and Louis Hall of Kahnawake, Johnny Cree of Kanasatake and reference to documents including Rev. Amand Parent's book on the Oka Indians, published in 1887.

July 12, (con't)

Ciaccia had arrived at Oka at 6:00 p.m. He met with members of the Warrior Society. They talked for nearly two-and-a-half hours. Mohawk tradition demands that peace talks and important negotiations take place only in the light of day. When the sun set, the talks were adjourned.

Ciaccia crossed back to the police side of the barricade and was taken by car to Montréal.

That left the Mohawk and the police alone to play their night time games of intimidation. Both sides sent men into the woods. They would creep along, sometimes in silence, sometimes making noise to let the other side know that the enemy was out there. The police shone powerful spotlights on the Mohawk.

Mirrors were brought out by the Mohawk and used to reflect the light back at the police.

For the Warriors, there would be no more than a few minutes sleep snatched here and there. The dancing lights, the shouts from the police side, the occasional war cry from the Mohawk and the steady sound of the insects and night birds continued through to the dawn.

Negotiation: Ciaccia with Mohawk negotiator Gabriel

Friday, July 13, 1990

It was Friday the 13th and the talks resumed behind the Mohawk barricades. Ciaccia told reporters that the negotiations were proceeding well and that he was "very optimistic" peace and order would soon be restored.

The Mohawk negotiators were less optimistic. They said that as long as Kanesatake was surrounded by the Sûreté du Québec, there could be no progress because the Mohawk would be too busy defending themselves and their land to deal with the technicalities of a negotiated settlement.

The only issue on which the two sides did agree upon was to keep the discussions private. No details would be announced to the press.

In fact, even without the news blackout, there would have been little to report. Ciaccia offered only a day-to-day moratorium on future police attacks. In return he demanded that the Kanesatake band instruct the Kahnawake Mohawk to lift their blockade of the Mercier Bridge.

The Mohawk rejected that plan. They believed that their control of the Mercier Bridge was the only bargaining chip they had. To give it up would be to give the police the green light to attack.

Kanesatake band spokesman Ellen Gabriel repeated her warning that the bridge would be blown up the moment the police began another assault on the barricades.

In Kahnawake, the Warriors said they would stand by their brothers and sisters from Kanesatake. The bridge could only be re-opened if the Sûreté du Québec was pulled out of the Oka region.

Another stumbling block to any settlement was the question of amnesty. The police said the killing of one of their men, the destruction of six police vehicles and the seizure of the bulldozer were criminal acts that could not go unpunished. But the Mohawk argued that what had taken place was an armed conflict between two nations – red and white – and that it was the white man who had started the war that left Corporal Marcel Lemay dead. The Mohawk, they said, were not to blame.

There was also the question of who shot Corporal Lemay. The Mohawk first claimed that he had accidently shot himself when he fell out of a tree and his gun went off. They later said he had been shot by one of his fellow officers in the confusion. It could not have been a Mohawk bullet, they argued, because the Warriors had been firing over the heads of their attackers.

The police said that story was false. They said Corporal Lemay was shot in the face or upper chest while he was moving forward toward the Mohawk line. They also said the Mohawk bullets were coming in at chest or eye level. Scars on the pine trees in the battle zone supported the police claim.

However, the Mohawk agreed to cooperate fully in any investigation into Lemay's death and Ellen Gabriel came forward with a message of condolence for the family of the slain officer.

At Chateauguay, just outside the Kahnawake reserve, protests against the Mohawk closing of the Mercier bridge began to turn violent. Mobs gathered on the police side of the barricades, taunting the Mohawk and screaming racist epithets.

Any Mohawk caught off the reserve became a target. But the first victims of the mob were whites. Two young white men entered a nearby supermarket where according to rumours, some Mohawk were attempting to buy food. The two were wearing army fatigue pants, and the mob mistook the pair for Mohawk Warriors. They were chased, caught and beaten before police arrived to rescue them. Both men were taken to hospital for treatment.

Sunday, July 15, 1990

Along the barricades, Mohawk and police remained locked in a tense, armed standoff. And the crowds of anti-Mohawk protesters in Chateauguay swelled.

But there was good news. Talks aimed at resolving the crisis were proceeding well. Officials of the Roman Catholic Church joined the negotiations as mediators. By evening, a tentative agreement had been reached.

Its main points were that the disputed land would go to the Mohawk, a public inquiry into the crisis would be held, and police would begin withdrawing from Oka. The withdrawal would be monitored by church groups. Under the terms of the agreement, Québec would support the Mohawk position that their talks with the federal government on the disputed land issue should be conducted on a "nation-to-nation" basis.

For their part, the Kanesatake band would ask the Kahnawake Mohawk to end their blockade of the Mercier Bridge. And once the police began to withdraw from Oka, the Mohawk would begin dismantling their barricades.

Both sides agreed that the standoff had gone on too long.

The Mercier Bridge would likely be opened within a day or two.

Warriors, guns, Molotov cocktails

Monday, July 16, 1990

The tentative agreement to resolve the crisis collapsed.

Québec Native Affairs minister John Ciaccia said the deal fell apart over "technicalities" which he would not specify. The Mohawk said there was only one

Debbie Etienne – The Day of the Battle

"Some of us women returned to the trees a few days before the army moved in. Dark sap was running down the big pines where the the bullet holes went in. It looked like the trees were crying. Those trees saved us though, just like Johnny Cree (spiritual spokesman) prayed for. We cried too because they were wounded."

"The actual attack started during the tobacco burning. We were up early, just about the whole village was there. At sunrise we were thanking the Great Creator for the sun and a new day. That's when the first shots and tear gas came in. The women went out to talk to them (the SQ). They wanted to talk to our leader. We told them the truth – that we had no leader – it was the people together that spoke. The officer couldn't grasp this and kept insisting he talk to our leader. We went back and asked Johnny Cree to talk to them. He is our faith keeper and hates the use of guns and any kind of violence.

"He told John they had orders to open fire if we all didn't leave the area so they could take down the barrier. Johnny said he would talk to us and when he came back he told us he thought it was more than just arrests they wanted. But we told him to tell them we were staying.

"Johnny went back and told them and asked that at least they give us time to finish our prayers so we would be prepared to meet our Creator. The SQ leader said we had five minutes then they were coming in. Johnny explained it would take longer than that. Then I think he gave us 45 minutes.

"All this time the women were making breakfast – sausages and scrambled eggs and peanut butter and jam sand-

The battle site

wiches. There was a lot of kids around and we just sort of did it to keep the kids happy and our minds occupied. When Johnny came back he almost pleaded with us to leave because he felt blood would be shed. Again we said 'No!' and asked Johnny to offer up a prayer. He prayed like this: 'Great Creator protect your

women and children and your people. Shelter the children, cover their eyes and ears to protect their hearts and minds. Whatever bad they send at us turn it back on them.' It was a lot longer than that but that was the basic idea.

"Then Turtle (Ellen Gabriel) started to burn sweetgrass. We went to the SQ lines and put the ash on them. They were scared. We put a line on the ground and asked that no enemy would cross it. Denise asked them 'Why do you want to kill me? Why do you want to kill my children?' That trooper slowly lowered his gun until his leader signalled him to reload and keep his weapon up. The girls spread out in a line.

"They yelled, 'Time is up. Are you going to leave?' We said, 'You know what our answer is. We cannot leave.' Then the concussion grenades and tear gas started. Soon after the bullets. The women started to run back.

"Our men were back in the bush behind the lacrosse rink. None of them had fired up to then because no order had been given. Around then there was a war cry given up to bring the Great Creator's attention to what was happening to us. When our men saw they (the SQ) were firing with women and children up front, the command to fire was given and they opened fire too. The youngest of the children was two and he was on a tricycle on the road. His little feet were peddling like heck. Bullets were kicking up dirt next to him. One of the men went out and grabbed him and pulled him behind a big pine. A woman was terrified and she fell. A warrior ran out and covered her with his body so he would take the bullets. The exchange lasted maybe five minutes but it seemed forever. Then I heard someone say, 'Look. They are running.' and the firing stopped."

"technicality" involved and that was the failure of the Québec government to withdraw the bulk of the 1,000-man police force surrounding the Kanesatake band.

As far as anyone could see, not a single police officer had been withdrawn.

On both sides of the barricades, there was a hardening of positions.

Mohawk spokesman Ellen Gabriel said that a partial withdrawal of the police would no longer be enough to end the blockade of the Mercier Bridge. All the police would have to go, she said, before the bridge could be re-opened.

The previous day, the police had allowed shipments of food and medicine to cross into the Mohawk land. Now, the police sealed off the reserve to even those vital goods.

You're violating our basic human rights, said the Mohawk.

Put down your weapons and all your rights will be respected, replied the authorities.

Tuesday, July 17, 1990

Chief Joe Norton of Kahnawake sent out an urgent appeal to Indian chiefs across Canada. Come to Kahnawake, he said, for an emergency meeting on the crisis. He said the Mohawk needed the support of all native people in order to convince Ottawa to get involved in the negotiations.

"I hope this will kick the federal government in the pants and get them moving," said Norton.

The federal minister for Indian Affairs, Tom Siddon, said that was not going to happen. He said federal intervention would only complicate the negotiations. The crisis is a provincial affair, he said, and Ottawa will stay on the sidelines.

But the Canadian armed forces said they expected to become involved. Forces' officials said they

were only waiting for the Québec police to formally call for help, and once that call came the military would move.

At Chateauguay, there was more violence on the police side of the barricades. A crowd of angry whites tried to force their way through the police lines in order to attack the Mohawk. The mob was beaten back by the police.

Wednesday, July 18, 1990

In Québec City, Premier Robert Bourassa called a press conference to deny stories that the Canadian army was preparing to intervene. He said that, for the time being, Québec was dealing with the crisis on its own and would continue to do so.

At Kanesatake, the Mohawk were waiting for the provincial Native Affairs minister, John Ciaccia. But he never showed up. He said the Mohawk had made it clear to him that they no longer had confidence in his ability to speak for all the parties concerned and that he was no longer welcome on Mohawk land.

At Kahnawake, the Mohawk negotiating team presented its new list of demands for taking down the barricades.

All negotiations, said the Mohawk must be carried out on the basis that the Mohawk are a free, sovereign and equal nation.

The police must begin withdrawing from Kanesatake and Kahanawake the moment the agreement is signed.

For 48 hours following the signing, all people must be permitted to leave the two Mohawk settlements without fear of arrest or having their cars searched.

Title to the disputed land at Oka should be given to the Kanesatake band.

And all other issues concerning the crisis should be put before the World Court at the Hague for resolution.

Friday, July 20, 1990

More than 100 Indian chiefs from across Canada gathered at Kahnawake to discuss native solidarity with the Mohawk. All urged the federal government to take part in the negotiations. But they warned that they would not stand

Chiefs gather at Kahnawake

Chief Oritz — The Christian Burial Ground

"Nothing more characterizes the Mohawk than their care for their dead."

"A short distance in back of Oka village lies the little Christian burying-ground of the remanent of Indians living on the Lake of Two Mountains. It was chosen with heed, and around the graves are evidences that fences had been erected to prevent the animals of the field paltry six feet in which his body rests when dead.

"The dark spot at the left of the picture shows the grave from which the body of the old Chief Oritz was taken and carried away after it had been placed there by the hands of his friends. He had defended his country in time of his grandchildren and great grandchildren were one by one hunted to jail for the crime of cutting what they considered to be their own wood.

"His was a sad end for an active life, a fitting emblem of the destruction of the race, once so powerful, of whom nothing will

The desecration of Chief Oritz' grave

from rudely trampling above those buried there. But these have been sawed and torn down by the enemies of the Indians and their religion, and it has been found impossible to protect the graves in any way. The spirit which prevented the Indian from fencing in his home and garden when living prevents his friends and family from claiming the need (War of 1812); and received special attention and honour at the hands of his King. During a full century of life he had experienced much change. In his youth he had been a warrior, courted by friends and dreaded by his enemies. He had searched for the lost Sir John Franklin expedition by way of the Mackenzie. Yet, during his latter days soon remain but the remembrance of the beautiful names they have given to our lakes, mountains, counties and streams."

From the book: The life of Rev. Amand Parent, and Eight Years among the Oka Indians. It was published in 1887.

by and watch the Mohawk be attacked. One chief said his band would bring down the power lines that carry electricity to Edmonton if police or the army moved against the Mohawk. Others promised to block rail lines or highways.

The chiefs also called on the international community to condemn Canada's federal government for its handling, or mishandling, of the crisis. And they asked the United Nations to appoint a commission to investigate Mohawk complaints that their political, civil, and human rights were being violated by the Québec police.

At Kanesatake, the Mohawk repeated their vow not to lay down their weapons as long as the police surrounded the settlement.

Although the federal government insisted that it would not become involved in the negotiations, rumours had circulated that Ottawa was attempting to buy the disputed land at Oka in order to hand it over to the Mohawk. Tom Siddon confirmed the rumours. The federal minister for Indian Affairs said Ottawa was close to acquiring the land. Funding for the purchase would come out of his ministry's budget for settling native land claims.

It was a plan the Mohawk did not embrace. Their argument was that the land was theirs anyway and that there would be no justice in using what was in effect Indian money to buy up Indian land.

Federal officials replied that they were bending over backward to accommodate the Mohawk and their efforts should be welcomed, not condemned.

Saturday, July 21, 1990

Talks between the Mohawk and the Québec government broke off completely with each side accusing the other of not showing good faith. The Mohawk said there could be no progress while hundreds of police officers were surrounding them and preventing their advisors from coming and going freely.

Québec said the main obstacle to progress was the refusal by the Mohawk leaders to come out from behind the barricades for peace talks. Native Affairs minister John Ciaccia said the talks could not take place inside an armed camp.

The Mohawk replied that they would not come out because they feared the police and did not have confidence in the minister's ability to control the Sûreté du Québec.

Despite the breakdown in the negotiations, the two sides continued to exchange proposals via intermediaries and fax machines.

Monday, July 23, 1990

John Ciaccia put forward a new plan to restart the negotiations. He said the Québec government would guarantee the safety and freedom of all Mohawk representatives going back and forth between Mohawk land and the negotiating site. The minister also accepted the Mohawk demand that observers be allowed to monitor events at the barricades. Those observers would be from human rights groups across Canada. And he promised that the Red Cross would not be hindered in its efforts to provide the Mohawk with adequate food and medical attention.

Again, the Mohawk replied that they did not like the idea of the talks taking place outside Mohawk territory. They also insisted that the observers be from outside Canada.

In Ottawa, the deputy minister of Indian Affairs, Harry Swain, described the Mohawk warriors as common criminals who were sabotaging the negotiating process.

Mohawk leaders said those kind of statements could only harm relations between their people and the Canadian authorities.

Tuesday, July 24, 1990

Federal officials urged both sides in the Mohawk crisis to continue their efforts aimed at restarting negotiations.

Senior members of the federal government, including Indian

Affairs minister Tom Siddon, refused to criticize deputy minister Harry Swain for his description of the Mohawk Warriors as criminals. Opposition members of parliament described Mr. Swain's remarks as ignorant, insensitive, and irresponsible.

In Québec, the leader of the opposition Parti Québecois, Jacques Parizeau, blasted the Liberal government of Premier Robert Bourassa. He said little had been done to end the long standoff. And he said it was time for Premier Bourassa to personally handle the negotiations.

Wednesday, July 25, 1990

The Mohawk were getting nervous. With the breakdown in the negotiations, they feared another police attack could come at any moment. The minister in charge of the provincial police force, Sam Elkas, did little to allay those fears when he announced that any future attack would include units from the armed forces. He also said there would be no negotiations with the Warriors some of whom, he claimed, were notorious criminals. Military officials said that although no formal call for help had come from Québec, some soldiers had already been moved to Montréal's Longue-Pointe Garrison.

The police were looking forward to the end of the standoff. They announced that they had opened hundreds of files on Mohawk who could be charged with criminal activites in relation to the crisis.

There was some good news for the Mohawk. Jean-Claude Fouque, the secretary general of the Paris-based International Human Rights Federation, arrived in Montréal to investigate allegations of human rights abuses

Chief Joseph Onasakenarat — Translator of the New Testement

When Methodist missionary Amand Parent (named Look to Heaven by the Mohawk) met Chief Joseph Onasakenarat in 1870 he described him as a fine, intelligent-looking Indian who was a born leader. Chief Joseph became the first man to translate the New Testament into Iroquois. Recognizing his leadership qualities the Suplicians sent him to school in Oka and then college in Montréal to prepare him for the priesthood. For a time, he was a professor of theology but became disillusioned with the Suplicians' treatment of the Mohawk. In 1868 his people asked him to be their chief after which he led them in demanding their rights from the Church:

"We have come to inform you first, that you have not dealt justly with us, and that we want you to leave our land, as we do not want to be robbed of our heritage; and you are yearly robbing us of the best of our property, therefore we would like to have it in more honorable hands.

"This land was given to you in trust for the tribe to whom it belongs; and how have you betrayed this trust? By selling the timber and filling your treasury with the proceeds of stolen property. This land is ours – ours by right of possession; ours as a heritage, given us as a sacred legacy. It is the spot where our fathers lie; beneath those trees our mothers sang our lullaby, and you would tear it from us and leave us wanderers at the mercy of fate."

CHIEF JOSEPH.

The church responded by demanding that Québec send an armed police force to arrest the dissidents. The provincial police force went to Oka and by force of arms imprisoned many of the Indians, including three chiefs. In prison, they were told by the brother of the bishop that unless they obeyed the priests he would have them shut up in Kingston Penitentiary for the rest of their lives. He informed Chief Joseph that the church had obtained some land in Doncaster, Ontario and they should all go there. Chief Joseph replied:

"We will never go there. To go there means extinction. We will not exchange a productive soil for barren rock in order to suit the whim of the pope. We will die on the land of our fathers, and our bleaching skeletons shall be a witness to nations yet unborn."

The Mohawk were charged with having the intention of killing the priests and driving them away. They were kept in jail in St. Scolastique for about seven days. It was during this period that Chief Joseph began his translation of the New Testament into Iroquois which had been forbidden by the Suplicians.

against the Mohawk. The federation represents 45 human rights groups from around the world. Mr. Fouque's invitation to visit the Mohawk came from the Québec Ligues des Droits et Libertes which said it believed the police were violating the rights of Mohawk under the Québec Charter of Human Rights.

Thursday, July 26, 1990

A senior official of the Québec government told reporters that the bullet which killed Corporal Marcel Lemay on July 11th did not come from a police weapon.

"It was a military-type projectile. The Sûreté does not use this type of projectile," said John McKenna, the chief of staff of Québec's solicitor-general Sam Elkas.

Mr. McKenna added that because the police only had the bullet, not the rifle from which it was fired, he could not say who fired the fatal shot.

But since the only people involved in the July 11th gunbattle were police and Mohawk, his statement made it plain that he believed it was a Mohawk who killed Cpl. Lemay.

At Kanesatake, the Mohawk were skeptical. They had said Cpl. Lemay was killed accidentally, either by his own men or by his own gun going off when he fell. The Mohawk said they had fired only over the heads of their attackers. And they insisted that only a ballistics test by a private, non-aligned laboratory would convince them otherwise.

At Kahnawake, Mohawk writer Johnny Beauvais said that as far as he was concerned, the question of where the bullet came from was immaterial.

"It was the conflict that killed the young man. It doesn't matter who fired the shot. The officer would have been alive if the police had not attacked," he argued.

The Mohawk counterattack also included a legal suit. Acting on behalf of the Kanesatake band, lawyer Eric Belhassen filed a motion for a class-action suit. He said the Sûreté du Québec was responsible for loss of income by Kanesatake residents stuck inside the barricades. The suit asked that the residents be paid compensation and that the police barricades be removed.

Federal Liberal leader Jean Chrétien

In Ottawa, Chief Billy Two Rivers of Kahnawake had a warning for the federal Liberal Party's committee on aboriginal affairs.

"We've been backed up into a corner," he said. "We can't back up anymore. When the first whites came to this country we offered our hand in peace. Don't force us to give it in the form of a fist."

The leader of the Liberal party, Jean Chretien, blasted the Progressive Conservative government and Indian Affairs minister Tom Siddon. Mr. Chretien said the minister had mishandled the land dispute which led to the violence at Oka, and had then refused to participate in negotiations to end the standoff.

Québec Native Affairs minister John Ciaccia sent a letter addressed to the Mohawk Nation at Kahnawake and Kanesatake. In it, he said Québec supports the efforts of the federal government to acquire the disputed land at Oka in order to give it to the Mohawk. He also said, for the first time, that Québec was willing to negotiate with all Mohawk representatives including members of the Longhouse, the body that controls the Warrior Society. And he offered to withdraw most of the police officers from Oka.

But in return, he demanded that the negotiations take place outside the barricades, that the Warriors surrender their weapons, and that the Mohawk take down their barricades at Kanesatake and Kahnawake.

Saturday, July 28, 1990

The Mohawk negotiating team replied to Mr. Ciaccia's proposal which it described as a disappointment. The Mohawk said the proposal still ignored their three main demands. Those were that food, water, clothing, bedding, and medical supplies be permitted to enter freely into Mohawk territory; that spiritual leaders, clan mothers, advisors and attorneys chosen by the Mohawk nation be given free access to Kanesatake; and that an international observer force made up of people from outside Canada be allowed to monitor the situation at Kanesatake and Kahnawake.

Later, the two sides talked by telephone. Mr. Ciaccia asked the Mohawk to reconsider their position and accept his proposal. The Mohawk asked the minister to grant their three demands.

No progress was made.

Sunday, July 29, 1990

The Mohawk sent another letter by fax machine to Mr. Ciaccia. It said the Mohawk wanted to ensure that there was no misunderstanding – the minister's proposal had not been rejected. But it hadn't been accepted either.

"Simply put," wrote the Mohawk, "it has not been considered and will not (be considered) until our three pre-conditions are met."

While the Mohawk were writing their letter, Mr. Ciaccia was writing one of his own to the Mohawk. In his letter, Mr. Ciaccia said that as far as he

was concerned the Mohawk preconditions had been met.

At Oka, more than 2,000 natives and non-natives held a rally in support of the Mohawk. But they were kept out of the town itself by local residents who set up a blockade of their own.

Kahnawake chief Joe Norton told the rally, "We will fight and die if we have to. We will arm ourselves and fight for our land if no one else will defend us."

Monday, July 30, 1990

The war of letters continued with the Mohawk replying to Mr. Ciaccia's claim that the preconditions had been met.

"We are pleased that you have agreed in principle to our first two preconditions. To say, however, that you have met them in practice, is another story. During the last few days, food stuffs, medicine and other necessary supplies have been stopped, delayed or tampered with. Moreover, necessary advisers and representatives of the Mohawk Nation were turned away by the Sûreté du Québec just last night."

The letter went on to say that concerning the third precondition – the demand for an international observer force – the Mohawk had demanded that the force be in place before formal negotiations could begin. And since no such force was yet in place, it could not be said that the precondition had been met.

Tuesday, July 3l, 1990

Oka town council voted unanimously not to sell the federal government the disputed

Johnny Cree — The Indian Community at Oka

Johnny Cree is 45, and father of four children. He lives in the house in Oka in which he was born and can trace some of his ancestors at Oka back seven generations. He is a spiritual faith keeper for the Longhouse and as such is against the carrying of arms. Neither does he favour any form of organized gambling on Indian land. He explained also that the way of the Longhouse is against the use of any substances such as drugs and liquor that alter the physical and mental state of the human body.

Questioned about the Pines, Johnny Cree said:

"The area of the Pines is our ceremonial place and sacred burial ground. We call it Onen'to: kon. It was our ancestors who had planted the trees all around. When I was young my parents and grandmother and grandfather took me there. It was there we played softball and lacrosse. It is our sacred place.

"Lacrosse is a ceremonial game. It tells us how to find a cure for illnesses and decides arguments. The way we play it, there could be a hundred on each side. I laugh when they say it is Canada's national game. It never was a white man's game. Canada has taken a lot of native things and ruined them. When Indians play lacrosse it is a rough game, a man's game. White men have turned it into a game for babies. They can't take the hits, they can't take the checks, they can't take the slashes. That game was not meant for Canadians. They should stick to hockey."

Do government incentives help?

"We don't like charity. We want to help ourselves. There is 85 percent unemployment among the Indians here. Programs are needed to build businesses for long-term employment that can offer medical benefits and old age pensions. Most of the government incentive

Lacrosse box at the Pines

programs last six months and there is altogether too much red tape attached. They tell us what we can do, where we can do it, and who we can sell to. All the bullshit kills the incentive and then the business fails. Anyway with the government setup right now the band council members take all the decent jobs for themselves."

What about a bingo hall?

"A bingo hall is not a business. There is no future in it. No education or special skills are needed to push cards or soft drinks. It pays kids minimum wages on a few nights a week and if it is run by outside interests, nothing comes back. That's why we fought it here. And it can be a bad influence on the community, too. Even if we did own it outright there would have to be restrictions on the type of gaming. No slots, craps, blackjack or roulette. If you are going to play bingo play bingo. Gambling itself changes and corrupts. It changes a calm community into a community that is possessed.

"I'm talking about real businesses like starting a lumber yard or a bowling alley, where a firm can employ so many people and offer reasonable wages and good fringe benefits. We have some plans for long-term jobs but first we have to get our land back. For example we would like to set up an Indian village in the (Paul Sauve) provincial park which is on our land. We would invite tourists to come and see the history of our people and show them what we believe in."

On drugs and alcohol, Johnny Cree has firm beliefs:

"People of the Longhouse do not believe in the use of alcohol or drugs in any way, shape or form. They do not belong in any society. Drugs bring violence,

murder, robbery. Alcohol will make people do things that they would not do in their right mind. But this is not just a native problem. Actually it has cut down a lot among our young people because there is pride. Our young are finding out who they are. There is no more shame. Even if our people in the TC get killed it won't stop the fight. The war will go on. Our people have nothing to be ashamed of. Those men in the TC center have done nothing wrong but defend the rights of the Iroquois nation and the lives of their women and children.

"The town of Oka and Québec and Canada are responsible for the violent act. They are the ones who have a lot of questions to ask themselves. I am completely against the use of arms but it has been very hard to stand by and watch the injustice and racism we experience every day. Can you see why we laugh when they tell us this is a democratic society? Politicians may know how to pronounce the word but they don't know how to live it. They should send Mr. Mulroney back to kindergarten to find out."

Federal Indian Affairs minister Tom Siddon

Wednesday, August 1, 1990

land which Ottawa wanted to buy in order to hand over to the Mohawk. It wasn't a question of price. The town said it would not sell the land until the Mohawk barricades came down. Ottawa had offered to pay $3.84 million for the 67 acres over which the crisis began. Oka would make a healthy profit in the deal. But the town said it wouldn't make any deals until the Mohawk laid down their arms.

In Paris, the International Federation of Human Rights began assembling a team of 24 observers to monitor the crisis at Oka and Kahnawake. Federation president Jean-Claude Fouque, who made an eight-day tour of the two Mohawk settlements, said he had found evidence of more than 50 human rights violations. In about half the cases, non-natives were the victims. Mohawk were the victims in the other cases.

And in Geneva, Kahnawake negotiater Kenneth Deer told the United Nations Human Rights Commission's committee on aboriginal people that the Mohawk crisis could easily turn into a "bloodbath."

The federal junior minister for Indian Affairs described the decision by Oka town council not to sell the disputed land to Ottawa as "regrettable but understandable."

"The federal offer to buy the land still stands," said Shirley Martin. "We trust that the Oka town council will soon be in a position to complete the transaction."

Ellen Gabriel – The Fine Art of Negotiating

Ellen Gabriel was born in Montréal in 1959. A Mohawk, she was raised at the Oka settlement where several generations of her family had grown up. Ellen is of the Turtle Clan and a member of the traditional Longhouse. A graduate of Concordia University with a degree in Fine Arts, Ellen was about to start teaching an adult education program in Oka when the crisis broke out. She had to put her plans on hold. Early in the negotiations, she was chosen by the women of the Longhouse to be a spokesman for the Kanesatake Mohawk.

During the crisis, Ellen became known for her soft-spoken but steadfast defense of Mohawk land claims. Afterward, she said that despite her bitter experiences and frustrating attempts to negotiate with the white authorities, she had no bad feelings towards Canadians in general. She said she believes they hold no ill will for the Mohawk.

"It is their leaders that I blame. I can't believe their ignorance."

And although the issues of Mohawk land claims and sovereignty were never settled, Ellen said she believed much good had come from the 78-day standoff.

"The people have renewed pride in themselves and I am very glad to see that. It proved that no matter what they did, they could not break our spirit".

In late October 1990, Ellen was one of a delegation of natives who travelled to Strasbourg, France to tell their story to the European Parliament.

"They treated us very well and were very sympathetic. They plan to send a non-partisan delegation to Oka to see things for themselves."

Another Mohawk named Gabriel who lived in Oka a hundred years ago was also a spokesman for his people. His story is told by missionary Amand Parent in his autobiography:

Parent describes Gabriel as "industrious, one of the better class of Indian". In 1873, writes the missionary, Gabriel refused to return to the Roman Catholic Church. He and many other Mohawk had converted to Methodism in part because they believed the Sulpicians were cheating them. Late one night, in the presence of his family, a bailiff took Gabriel from his one-room home to jail. There, he was visited by a priest and offered his freedom if he would go back to the church of Rome. It would be an example to other Indians. But the Mohawk was adamant. He said he would rather die.

Eventually he was freed. Soon after his release, he began to rebuild his one room home in preparation for winter. For this he needed lumber. On the pretext that he had cut wood without the church's permission, he was again jailed. In fact, he had paid the priest a sum of money in advance to cut the trees he needed. While in jail, he contracted pneumonia. By the time he was released, it was winter and he had to walk from Ste. Scolastique through the snow to Oka. His poor house was little shelter from the cold and he died at home eight days later. But to the end he had been a thorn in the side of the Sulpicians.

In Ottawa, Kahnawake traditional chief and band council member Billy Two Rivers called on the Senate to help resolve the Mohawk crisis.

Speaking to a Senate committee on aboriginal affairs, he said there would be "nothing but turmoil, chaos, and confrontation for the future" if the crisis was not resolved peacefully. He said that could come about only if the Canadian government gained a better understanding of what the Mohawk nation is all about.

Thursday, August 2, 1990

Québec Premier Robert Bourassa announced that anyone who had suffered financial loss as a result of the standoff between police and Mohawk would be eligible for compensation. Those who could expect to receive cheques from Québec City included Oka residents who had fled their homes, businesses that had been shut down by the dispute, and commuters forced to drive hundreds of extra kilometers each week because of the closing of the Mercier Bridge.

The premier said it was "normal that the government do whatever can be done to help those people."

Sunday, August 5, 1990

Premier Bourassa said the standoff had gone on long enough. And he presented the Mohawk with an ultimatum. Lay down your weapons and begin negotiations within 48 hours, he said, or the government would take

Québec Premier
Robert Bourassa

Chief Billy
Two Rivers

Canadian Prime Minister
Brian Mulroney

"appropriate steps." The premier would not say what those steps would be. But he would not rule out a military or police assault on the Mohawk barricades. The premier said the provincial government had accepted the main points of the Mohawk preconditions for peace talks but that the tentative agreement had been scuttled by Mohawk intransigence. The Mohawk argued that their preconditions – including the demand that an observer force be made up only of foreign nationals – were the minimum they could accept.

Monday, August 6, 1990

The Mohawk at Kanesatake said they would not be swayed by Premier Bourassa's 48-hour ultimatum.

Spokesman Joe Deom described the ultimatum as "a threat to negotiate under the gun."

And negotiator Ellen Gabriel said the Mohawk intended to wait for the premier's deadline to pass before going on with efforts to find a negotiated settlement to the crisis.

But they did agree to drop demands that the peace talks also include such issues as Mohawk grievances at the Akwesasne reserve, part of which lies on the United States side of the frontier.

The negotiating committee sent a letter to Prime Minister Brian Mulroney asking him, once again, to join in the negotiating process. The letter said the provincial minister of Native Affairs, John Ciaccia, claimed he did not have the power to implement any of the Mohawk preconditions. Therefore, said the Mohawk, it appeared to them that only Prime Minister Mulroney himself had the authority to get things moving.

Signs of divisions among the Mohawk appeared, however, undermining their strength at the bargaining table. George Martin, the grand chief of the Kanesatake band and the head of the local band council, described the Mohawk Warriors at Kanesatake as an "occupying force." And he called for them to leave immediately.

"No matter how noble the cause to prevent a golf course expansion on ancestral land and burial grounds, violence and intimidation can never be accepted," he said.

Tuesday, August 7, 1990

In Kanesatake, the Mohawk believed an assault, probably led by the army was coming. Some packed up their belongings, locked their homes, and left the area. Others chose to stay in the community. The local community center – which was already being used as a food bank for the Mohawk – was turned into an emergency shelter with room for 150 people to sleep.

In Kahnawake, Mohawk negotiators led by traditional chiefs Joe Norton and Billy Two Rivers again accused the provincial government of blocking progress toward a negotiated settlement. They also accused the police of preventing food and desperately needed medicine from entering the two Mohawk settlements. Québec officials denied the charges.

Wednesday, August 8, 1990

Prime Minister Mulroney announced that the Canadian armed forces would be sent to Oka and Kahnawake where they would replace RCMP and Québec police. The decision to send in the army came at the request of Québec premier Robert Bourassa who was also in power the last time the army was called to restore order in Québec. That was during the October Crisis of 1970.

The prime minister used the carrot-and-stick approach. While announcing that the army would move in, he also said that Alan B. Gold, a chief justice of the Québec Superior Court, had been given a mandate to negotiate with the Mohawk.

Mr. Mulroney would not say whether the armed forces would be given orders to attack the Mohawk barricades. But he did say he would not describe the miltary's mission as a peacekeeping operation.

On the Mohawk side, there were mixed feelings. Most Mohawk were glad to hear that the hated Sûreté du Québec would be replaced by the soldiers. The Mohawk believed the soldiers would be more disciplined and would not be out for revenge. But they also believed that the army would be much more difficult to defeat in an armed confrontation. And they feared that the army had been called in for the sole reason of launching a full military assault against their positions.

However, they decided to take a wait-and-see position. There would be no concessions made as a result of the prime minister's announcement. And Mohawk women and children would remain behind the barricades.

"We are the ones who have been invaded,"said Chief Billy Two Rivers who added that the Mohawk wanted to co-exist with the dominant white society – but not at any price.

The Mohawk believed that when they woke up the next morning, they would see the army in all its might spread out on the other side of their barricades.

Thursday, August 9, 1990

When dawn broke at Kahnawake and Kanesatake, there was no sign of the armed forces. But the police were still there.

Later in the day, Canadian Forces Lieutenant-General Kent Foster announced that it would still be a while before his troops took up positions at the barricades. He said the Forces and the federal government both wanted to give federal negotiator Alan Gold time to find a peaceful solution to the conflict. The presence of armed soldiers at Kanesatake and Kahnawake, he said, could be disruptive to those negotiations. But he warned that if no progress was made at the bargaining table, the army would be ready to move in by early in the week.

Mercier Bridge from Kahnawake

Louis Hall — The High Steel Workers

The Indian word for the Six Nations is Rotinonsonni which is generally pronounced as Hau-de-no-sau-nee. It is the proper word for the people of the Longhouse and means people who build the house. The Mohawk's ancestors were builders of sturdy wooden houses, then quarry miners and stone workers, and later steel workers. They were always interested in mastering any building job and when stone construction gave way to steel construction in the 20th century, the Mohawks became the best practitioners of the skill. Because New York was an employment centre for high steel workers, the largest settlement of Mohawk outside Québec is Brooklyn, New York.

"I used to sell stone. I would make something the shape of a wood cord 4X4X8 of large pieces of stone. We sold it to builders for $4.00. At first it took me ten hours but I got it down to four. There was one piece of stone that weighed 500 lbs. Nobody would carry it away so it stayed as the corner of my cord. I wanted to learn how to lay stone so I went to help a real good stone worker, Pete Mayo. We were laying stone one day when I noticed the great stone laying there. I wondered who had managed to lift it. Then Pete just picked up the stone and laid it like any other. I did a double take, he was the strongest man I ever knew. In the fall Pete Mayo always left to rig steel in New York.

"It was Peter Rice, a Mohawk from Kahnawake who got the Mohawk into high steel work all over the world. This is how it happened. In 1929, the Empire State Building was six months behind schedule. Rice had a good reputation for getting the job done so the construction company asked him to supervise the building of this 102-storey building. He said he would do it only if he could

bring his own crew. So Rice brought 200 Mohawks to New York and not only caught up the job but finished it a year ahead of schedule. That was in 1931.

"This established the Mohawk's reputation as the best

Bruemmer photo

steel workers in the business. A couple of years later it was decided to build the Mercier Bridge across the St Lawrence. Dominion Bridge was the contractor and hired mostly Mohawk to do the job.

"They already had hired

most of the supervisors, so Pete got the job as boss of the strippers (the workers who stripped off the wooden forms around the freshly-laid concrete). About the time the bridge was completed (1934), Peter's cousin, who was also called Peter Rice, was in San Francisco working on the Golden Gate bridge. He sent word that the owners would hire good steel men. Jobs were scarce so all the men left in a hurry. It was depression time and money was hard to come by, but the men crossed the country under freight trains, riding the rods. It took four days without food and sleep because it was easy to fall under the wheels if you didn't stay awake. In San Francisco, many were hired and worked there till the bridge was finished in 1937. But so many had showed up for work they ran out of jobs. However, the owners of the construction company building the bridge also had a contract to build new eight-hundred-foot towers for the locks on the Panama Canal.

"So the balance of the men from Kahnawke just kept moving on down the continent another couple of thousand miles until they reached Panama."

For residents of Chateauguay, that was not the news they wanted to hear. A month of long detours caused by the blockade of the Mercier Bridge had left many residents of the south shore suburb impatient for action. They wanted the army to move in as quickly as possible.

The Québec minister of public security, Sam Elkas, attempted to mollify them somewhat by announcing that construction would begin immediately on a new highway bypassing the Kahnawake reserve and the Mercier Bridge.

Friday, August 10, 1990

Federal mediator Alan Gold went behind the barricades at Kanesatake for talks with the Mohawk. Afterward, he would give no word on how the talks had progressed – or had not progressed. The Mohawk, too, agreed to a news blackout. But they did say they were happy that Justice Gold, and by extension, the federal government, had become involved in the efforts to seek a peaceful and fair settlement to the crisis.

However, they feared that Ottawa expected Justice Gold to use the presence of the armed forces as a tool with which to hammer concessions out of the Mohawk.

Forces officials said the soldiers would not move in until Justice Gold gave the go-ahead. And to the Mohawk negotiators, that sounded like a veiled threat not to argue with the mediator.

The department of National Defense in Ottawa tried to allay those fears by saying the negotiations and the possible military intervention were two separate issues. Justice Gold, it said, would have no say in deciding when or if the military would move.

Saturday, August 11, 1990

Premier Bourassa met with police and military officials at St. Jean Port Joli. The meeting was called by the premier and the military commanders to discuss the possibility of military intervention at Kahnawake and Kanesatake. Mr. Bourassa wanted to know how the armed forces would move against the Mohawk barricades, what kind of casualties could be expected, and how sure the military could be of success.

The talks were held behind closed doors without any advance notice and with no word of the results. But news of the meeting quickly leaked out. And it once again led to rumours that the military was preparing to attack, perhaps within 24 hours.

Sunday, August 12, 1990

It looked as if peace was coming. Federal Indian Affairs minister Tom Siddon and his provincial counterpart, John Ciaccia, went to Kanesatake to sign a treaty with representatives of the Mohawk nation. The signing ceremony took place in the Pines behind the Mohawk barricades near the spot where Corporal Marcel Lemay was shot dead on July 11th. Signing for the Mohawk were, among others, Warriors wearing masks. They used traditional Mohawk names for the ceremony.

It was a victory for the Warriors. Under the terms of the accord, the federal and provincial authorities agreed to all three of the Mohawk preconditions for formal peace talks.

Those preconditions were: the free passage of food, medicine, and other necessities into Kanesatake and Kahnawake; full access to legal and spiritual advisers; and the establishing of an international observer force made up entirely of non-Canadians and appointed by the Paris-based International Federation of Human Rights.

The governments had also given into the Mohawk demand that the negotiating and signing of the three-point agreement take place on the Mohawk side of the barrier.

In Chateauguay, there was no rejoicing. Protestors, angry that the Mercier Bridge had now been closed for more than a month, blocked a bridge across the St. Lawrence Seaway near Valleyfield. Police in riot gear moved in to clear the bridge, and the confrontation quickly turned violent. The police used clubs to beat back the protesters. One police officer was thrown off the bridge. Others were hit by rocks and bottles. Several people were arrested. Later, a mob gathered outside the police station where the arrested protesters were being held. Greatly outnumbered, the police could only stand by as the mob smashed windows and damaged police cars parked outside.

That night, violence broke out once again at the Chateauguay barricades. It began with demonstrators shouting insults at the police. Then some eggs and tomatoes were thrown at the officers. When that failed to get much of a reaction, some members of the crowd dug up paving bricks from the side of the road. Dozens of the bricks rained down on the police who, taken by surprise, fell back 15 meters. They quickly regrouped and fired tear gas into the crowd. Then they charged into the demonstrators. It was all over within a few minutes. The police had reclaimed their barricades, and the crowd thinned out as people fled the stinging smoke of the tear gas. There were injuries on both sides. And it left the police officers wondering what they were doing at the barricades and who they were defending.

Monday, August 13, 1990

Québec Native Affairs minister John Ciaccia announced that formal negotiations between the government and the Mohawk would begin the next day now that the three-point pact had been signed. The talks, he said, would take place behind closed doors.

Some Mohawk were critical of the signing. They argued that the five Mohawk who signed the document were not traditional chiefs, did not sign their usual names, and had little right to negotiate on behalf of the Mohawk nation.

Chief Tom Porter of the Mohawk Nation Council at Akwesasne said those who signed had never been given any sort of mandate by the Mohawk

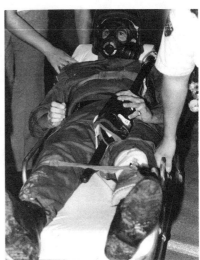

people to negotiate on their behalf. But others said council members such as Mr. Porter were out of touch with the Mohawk people and had lost their right to speak on behalf of the Mohawk nation.

In Chateauguay, only a few hundred people turned out for the nightly anti-Mohawk demonstration. However, among the crowd were dozens of young men who had come ready for a battle. After the usual insults had been screamed at the police, the men began throwing rocks and molotov cocktails. This time, the police were prepared. They charged after their tormentors. For two hours, they chased demonstrators through the streets of Chateauguay. When it was over, some two dozen people were under arrest. But, perhaps miraculously, nobody was seriously injured.

Tuesday, August 14, 1990

At the request of the Québec government, the Canadian Forces began moving 2,500 troops closer to Kahnawake and Kanesatake.

Military officials said the troops were being brought forward so that they would be able to move quickly in the event they were needed – but there were no plans to move the soldiers to the barricades in the coming days.

The movement came as peace talks between the Mohawk and the authorities appeared set to resume. For the Mohawk, word of the army's movements appeared to be aimed at strengthening the hand of the government negotiators. But the white authorities denied the accusation. They said the military had its own agenda independent of the negotiating process.

For the third consecutive night, there were violent confrontations between police and anti-Mohawk mobs in Chateauguay.

Chief Joe Norton — for Peace and Dignity

The challenge for Kahnawake Grand Chief Joe Norton was to prevent any blood from being spilled on the reserve while at the same time not giving ground in the fight for Mohawk autonomy.

It was a fine line he walked throughout the crisis. To succeed, Norton had to be radical enough to convince the Warriors that he would not sell them out and moderate enough to win the confidence of the white negotiators.

From the time the barriers went up on July 11th to their dismantling on August 29th, not a shot was fired at Kahnawake. Norton had succeeded.

But the challenge of maintaining peace and dignity remained even after the blockades had been removed. Police and army raids, the trashing of Mohawk homes by police searching for weapons, and the decisions by the Sûreté du Québec to resume patrols of the highways passing through Kahnawake infuriated the people of the reserve. For Norton, there would be no end to his efforts to keep the situation from exploding.

This time, the demonstrators added golf balls to their arsenal of firebombs, bottles, tomatoes, and rocks. A dozen police officers were injured by the objects. And at least one of the demonstrators was seriously hurt when he was hit in the face by a rifle-fired tear gas cannister.

The policemen on the lines were quickly running out of patience. Many of the more violent protestors appeared to be out there only because they enjoyed the novelty of pelting police officers with rocks and other missiles. The police union threatened to withdraw the officers if something was not done to improve the situation.

Wednesday, August 15, 1990

Teams of observers appointed by the Paris-based International Federation of Human Rights took up positions at Kahnawake and Kanesatake. And the Mohawk agreed that they would bring no weapons and would wear no masks at the Dorval Hilton where peace talks were scheduled to begin the following day.

Some Mohawk, however, were worried. Traditional chief George Martin of Kanesatake said he feared the Warriors would take over the negotiations. Many of the Warriors at Kanesatake came from other Mohawk communities. They should not be the ones to decide the future of the Kanesatake lands, Mr. Martin argued.

From the early days of the crisis, Mr. Martin had been in conflict with the Warriors. He said they had threatened him and that they were using brute force to usurp the band council's legitimate leadership of the community. But many members of the community disagreed. They said the defense of their land was paramount, and it was the time to show unity, not dissension.

At Chateauguay, police tried a new tactic to stop the nightly riots. Instead of standing in a line at their barricades, they moved in groups of twos and threes among the crowd. By doing so, they no longer presented a solid, inviting target for the demonstrators' rocks and firebombs. At the same time, the rock-throwers could not avoid arrest by hiding behind the front ranks of the crowd. The tactic was a success. There was no violence.

Thursday, August 16, 1990

The peace talks finally began. But they immediately became bogged down over the issue of who was negotiating for the Mohawk. Three people

were to negotiate for the Mohawk side. At least, that's what the federal and provincial authorities expected. They came to the table with three people in each delegation. But when the Mohawk negotiating team arrived at the Dorval Hilton, there were 54 of them.

For much of the rest of the day, the two sides engaged in bickering. The white authorities argued that it would be impossible to negotiate with 54 people. They accused the Mohawk of deliberately undermining the process. The Mohawk answered that their tradition calls for such important issues to be decided by consensus – not by a few.

At the end of the day, the Mohawk gave into the pressure and agreed to choose five people to represent them at the talks. They insisted, though, that the five be allowed to consult with the other Mohawk and advisors throughout the negotiations.

Both sides agreed to a news blackout.

Going into the talks, the chief negotiator for Québec, Alex Paterson, announced that he was ready to work night and day to achieve a negotiated settlement as quickly as possible. The Mohawk told him he'd be working the nights without them. Mohawk tradition dictates that negotiations be carried out in the light of day.

At Kanesatake, the first formal complaint was filed with the international observers. The Mohawk said a group of soldiers dressed in camouflage gear had infiltrated behind Mohawk lines. Such actions, they said, could easily lead to an unwanted and violent confrontation. The armed forces denied that any soldiers had been in the area. And the Mohawk could produce no proof for the observer team.

Friday, August 17, 1990

The Canadian Armed Forces announced that as many 4,400 soldiers backed by armored personnel carriers and heavy weapons would replace the police at Kanesatake and Kahnawake. Military officials said the forces' mission would be to restore order to the two communities and that the goal would be to accomplish that mission without any violence.

All military moves, they said, would be conducted out in the open. The press and the Mohawk would be given advance warning of each operation.

Army Strength

The Canadian Forces sent the 5th Mechanized Brigade to Kanesatake and Kahnawake at the request of Québec Premier Robert Bourassa. The brigade was under the command of Brigadier-General J.A. Roy.

One of the regiments employed was Canada's oldest, The Royal Canadian Regiment (The RCR's) which was formed in 1883. The first of the many battle honours it won in five wars was awarded for The Battle of Cut Knife Creek and the capture of Louis Riel in Saskatchewan in 1885.

Also called up for duty was the Royal 22nd Regiment (Vandoos), Canada's most famous French-speaking infantry regiment. The Vandoos have a distinguished battle record through both World Wars and the Korea conflict. Here is an inventory of manpower and weaponry.

UNITS EMPLOYED

Infantry:	2nd Battalion of The Royal Canadian Regiment (The RCR's)	Military Police:	5th Military Police Platoon
		Service Corps:	5th Canadian Service Battalion
	2nd and 3rd Battalions of the Royal 22nd Regiment (the Vandoos)	Medical Corps:	5th Field Ambulance unit.
Artillery:	5th Lt. Artillery Regiment	Air Force:	Fighter Squadron, Cold Lake 430 Tactical Helicopter Squadron
Armoured:	12th Armoured Regiment	Navy:	CSV 'Acadian' (navigation and reconnaissance)
Engineers:	5th Field Combat Engineers		

Total Strength: 3,300 officers and men

Weapons and equipment

Soldier with C8

M113. APC

105 mm

Small arms :
Infantry soldiers are armed with C7s and C8s. The C7 is a semi-automatic rifle modified from the US M16 for cold weather combat. Its 30-round magazine fires .556 NATO compatible ammunition. The C8 is a Belgian-made light (.556) calibre fully automatic machine gun with a 200-round magazine.

Armoured personnel carriers (APCs) :
Grizzlys, Cougars, Lynx, Dozers and M113s. These amphibious troop carriers can be tracked or wheeled and are armed with

.50 calibre armour-piercing machine guns, grenade launchers (Grizzlys) and/or 76 mil cannons capable of firing high explosive or smoke shells (Cougars). Lynx are armoured reconnaisance vehicles and tracked M113s can be fitted with bulldozer blades for barricade removal.

Artillery :
105mm self-propelled field artillery pieces.

Tanks :
Three high-tech Leopard tanks, made in Germany.

Helicopters :
Squadron of 20 Huey (troop carrying), and Kiowa (reconnaissance) helicopters.

Fighter Planes :
2 CF5s (Freedom Fighters). Mostly used for training in Canadian Air Force.

Ships :
CSV. 'Acadian'. 50 ft. naval reserve observation craft used in navigation training.

Kiowa

Cougar APC

Grizzly APC

Leopard tank

Sunday, August 19, 1990

The negotiators took the day off. It was a chance to rest after the intense bargaining sessions and to assess the progress that had been made so far. Both sides respected the agreement not to disclose to the press what had gone on behind the closed doors. But there were hints from both camps that things had gone well and that the major issues – including the Kanesatake land dispute that sparked the crisis – were close to resolution. The Mercier Bridge, said some sources, would likely be opened within the next week.

At the barricades, the police were preparing to hand over control to the army. It would be a case of "goodbye and good riddance" all around. The Mohawk detested the Sûreté du Québec and would not miss their presence. The residents of Chateauguay and the other south shore suburbs surrounding Kahnawake had fought with riot police on numerous occasions. They were angry that the police had used clubs on their own people rather than on the Mohawk. And the police were tired of being pelted by rocks and bottles thrown by the whites and by the insults hurled at them from behind the Mohawk lines.

Monday, August 20, 1990

The army moved in. At 8:00 a.m., columns of soldiers in armored personnel carriers began arriving at the police barricades around Kahnawake and Kanesatake. Four-hundred soldiers were deployed at Kahnawake while 335 troops took up positions at Oka. The police left almost immediately.

The metal crowd-control barriers set up by the police were quickly replaced by concrete barriers and concertina razor-wire. The APCs with their .50-calibre machine guns were dug in at strategic positions along the line.

At Chateauguay, a small group of soldiers walked forward toward the Mohawk lines. Two Mohawk Warriors came out to meet them. For 10 minutes, the men stood in no-man's land and talked. The soldiers explained what positions they would be holding. The Warriors said they could live with those positiones but warned the soldiers that any sudden movements into the demilitarized zone could spark a gunbattle. Each side agreed that it understood the other. The soldiers shook hands with the Warriors and the two groups turned and went back to their respective barricades.

At Oka, things were not going as smoothly. One of the police barricades along the northern perimeter had been set up at the bottom of a hill. From that position, the military was at a tactical disadvantage. The soldiers could not see much of the Mohawk defenses and the Mohawk would have an ideal line of fire down on the troops. The two lines were nearly a kilometer apart, and when the army took over from the Sûreté du Québec, it moved the barricade forward 400 meters.

The already-nervous Mohawk defenders at first feared the soldiers would not stop coming forward. Military officials said the Mohawk had been given advance warning, but the Mohawk at the Kanesatake barricades said they had not heard anything of the army plan. They described the action as an act of aggression.

The peace talks were scheduled to resume at 10:00 a.m. at a nearby Trappist monastery. When the government negotiators arrived, they found no Mohawk there with whom to negotiate. Angered by the military encroachment into the demilitarized zone, the Mohawk refused to talk. The government team waited two hours and then went home.

Telephone calls were made and a military helicopter was sent to Kahnawake to pick up members of the negotiating team. They were flown to Oka where they held a conference with the military and the Warriors. The meeting took place in the middle of Oka's main street halfway between the Mohawk and army lines.

Nearly one hour after the talks had begun, the Mohawk negotiators said they were satisfied with the army's promise not to move any farther forward for the time being. The negotiations, they announced would resume the next day.

Throughout the rest of the day, the soldiers spent their time putting up tents, filling and stacking sand bags, and stringing up communication lines. By evening, the military was prepared for a long – or short – stay at Kahnawake and Kanesatake.

On the Mohawk side of the barricades, there was little for the Warriors to do but watch the soldiers and wait for something to happen.

Tuesday, August 21, 1990

The peace talks began again at the Oka monastery. When the talks adjourned three days earlier, both sides had suggested that a resolution to the crisis was in sight. But that optimism fizzled soon after the talks reopened. The Mohawk began by putting forward a three-point proposal that greatly extended the scope of the bargaining.

The first point called for the ownership of the disputed land at Kanesatake to be given to the Mohawk nation. Since the federal government had already let it be known it was purchasing the land for just that purpose, this point caused little problem.

The second point, however, called on the authorities to agree to the creation of a unified Mohawk nation to be known as Kanienkahaka. It would be made up of the six Mohawk communities in Québec, Ontario and New York state. All disputes, such as land claims and issues relating to Mohawk sovereignty, would be negotiated by Kanienkahaka as a whole. The government negotiators were furious. How, they asked, could Québec unilaterally accept such a condition when it also affected the province of Ontario and the United States?

Point three demanded that the Québec authorities stop prosecutions in connection with the high-stakes bingo hall at Kahnawake. The parlor offered jackpots five times higher than those allowed under Québec law. Although the police had yet to raid the hall, they frequently arrested whites leaving the bingo parlor. Those charged had their winnings seized. Once the arrests began, many patrons stopped going to the reserve.

The government negotiators knew they would have a hard time selling the Mohawk proposal to Premier Robert Bourassa. From the start, he had maintained that there could be no waiving of any laws for the Mohawk.

When the talks ended for the evening, there were no more words of hope coming from the government negotiating team.

At the barricades in Oka and Chateauguay, dozens of armored vehicles and hundreds more soldiers arrived. The army now had 1,400 troops deployed around the two Mohawk communities.

In LaSalle at the northern end of the Mercier Bridge, a new barricade went up. Under the August 12th preliminary agreement signed by the

Big John Canadian — A Mercy Mission to Khartoum

Big John, a Mohawk from Kahnawake, was the first man to pilot a steamer through the Lachine Rapids. Thereafter he frequently piloted commercial and pleasure craft through these dangerous waters of the St. Lawrence. He and his fellow Mohawk became world famous for their skills at riding white water.

In 1884, in the Sudan city of Khartoum, part of the British Army under General Gordon was besieged by the Arabs. Gordon had held out for months without supplies or rein- forcments. It was certain that Khar- toum would soon fall to the dreaded Mahdi (the leader of the Arab revolt). The British gov- ernment had balked at sending back-up troops because of petty politics. Khartoum was strategically situated near the joining of the White and Blue Nile but the cataracts of the Nile were con- sidered unnavigable, making it

difficult to get reinforcements there in a hurry. Finally the Brit- ish decided to act. At the request of Lord Wolsley who com-

manded the British army in Af- rica, Louis Jackson – a Mohawk – brought Big John as leading pilot and 52 of his Mohawk brothers to Eygpt. Their task

would be to pilot troop-carrying boats through the 'impassable' cataracts of the Nile to relieve Gordon. Despite impossible odds, Big John and his boys got the troops through. Two Mohawk were lost in the extraor- dinary feat.

Unfortunately for the British they were two days late. The garrison had fallen and Gordon had died with all his men. This in no way should undermine the achievement of the Mohawk. No one before or in the hundred years since has conquered the cataracts of the Nile.

Mohawk and the governments, the Mohawk were guaranteed the right to travel between Kahnawake and Kanesatake. To do so, they were travelling by car across the Mercier Bridge. The idea that Mohawk were using the bridge that was closed to white commuters did not sit well with some whites. They put up a barricade of their own to prevent any Mohawk from crossing.

Wednesday, August 22, 1990

Québec public security minister Sam Elkas accused the Mohawk of negotiating in bad faith.

"We were supposed to discuss the dismantling of barricades. That's what we agreed to when we signed the three preconditions," he said referring to the August 12th agreement.

By bringing the issues of Mohawk nationhood and bingo to the bargaining table, argued Mr. Elkas, the Mohawk had broken faith with the pact.

The Mohawk responded that, as usual, they had been misunderstood. Neither the bingo question or the issue of a unified Mohawk nation were meant to be taken as preconditions for the lifting of the Mohawk blockades.

Dock on Ciaccia's property

Trappist monastery at Oka

Instead, the Mohawk were asking for confirmation that those issues would be addressed at some time in the future.

The peace talks continued behind closed doors at the Oka monastery. With the news blackout in effect, neither side would say what took place inside. The federal and provincial negotiators did, however, suggest that the process was at least moving in the right direction.

In Dorval, police were called out when a crowd of whites, some of them armed with baseball bats, attempted to stop Kahnawake residents from ferrying supplies across the river by small boat. The Mohawk of Kahnawake were bringing food and fuel from the island to their blockaded reserve. And the boats were tying up at a small wooden dock built on a Dorval property owned, ironically, by Québec's minister of Native Affairs, John Ciaccia.

In Montréal, Premier Robert Bourassa attempted to pacify a crowd of angry Chateauguay residents demonstrating in front of his office. He promised that if negotiations did not produce a settlement in the coming days his government would consider "other options" to bring down the barricades.

Since the only other option appeared to be military force, the Mohawk took the statement as another warning that time was running out.

On the outskirts of Oka, police used force to turn back a group of 18 native veterans who had fought for Canada during the Second World War. The group had travelled to Oka to show their support for the Mohawk cause.

Thursday, August 23, 1990

The army moved forward. And the Mohawk broke off negotiations. Throughout the standoff, the Mohawk and the police lines had been separated by a stretch of no-man's land up to 1.5 kilometers wide. Now the army was closing that gap. And at Kanesatake, the soldiers began setting up their razor-wire fences just five meters away from some of the Mohawk defenses.

For a while, it appeared that the Warriors would fire on the advancing soldiers. But eventually, calm was restored and the soldiers and Warriors contented themselves with glaring contests.

By late afternoon, the Mohawk announced that they would return to the peace talks.

"If this isn't negotiating at the point of a gun, I don't know what the hell is," said Kahnawake chief Joe Norton. "I guess if we have to negotiate with guns to our heads then we have to negotiate with guns to our heads. We're not going to be the ones to walk away from the table."

Mavis Etienne — Spiritual Freedom

Mavis Etienne, a Mohawk Indian, is an outreach counsellor at the Drug and Alcohol Rehabilitation Center at Kanesatake. It was the center, or TC, taken over by the Warriors for their final standoff with the army.

"The Center's proper Indian name is Onen'to:kon. It means 'under the pines'. We have been open for four years and have had very good results. Natives from all over Québec are eligible for treatment here. We started cleaning up immediately after the army left and the centre was operational again within two weeks.

"My father was born in Oka, his name was Morris Cree. He was a Methodist and belonged to the old Methodist church started in Oka in 1870. In 1922 he joined the Pentecostal church. My great-grandfather was a Cree from Manitoba and he came to Oka and married a Mohawk girl in the late 1800s.

"Under the law of the Iroquois Confederacy, religious thought is free. I remain faithful to traditional Mohawk ways as taught through The Great Law of Peace. I am also a born-again Christian and find no conflict with the Christian Bible and the Longhouse concept of the Great Creator. It is how we mediate with God that is a little different. I choose to do it through Christ."

Mrs. Etienne was a member of the Mohawk negotiating team for almost two months. She was not present in the Pines on the morning of July 11th. But on August 26th, she was arrested by the SQ who claimed she had been there. She asked them for their evidence. She says they produced a photograph showing her with the Secretary-General of the International Human Rights Federation, as she escorted him to the negotiating table – an event that took place weeks later.

Friday, August 24, 1990

The negotiations resumed with both sides presenting their latest proposals. But the Mohawk were bitter. They said the army's decision to move troops right up to the Warriors' barricades at Oka threatened to lead to bloodshed. And they warned that they could withdraw from the talks if police did not take measures to ensure that negotiators from Kahnawake could make their way to the site of the negotiations at Oka. Groups of whites armed with baseball bats and chains had been preventing anyone from driving out of the Kahnawake reserve.

When the talks adjourned at the end of the day, however, the Mohawk negotiators were more cheerful. Chief Joe Norton said "substantive" progress had been achieved and he was confident an agreement would soon be reached. Even the chief Québec negotiator, Alex Paterson, went as far as to say the two sides were "quite close" to a negotiated end to the crisis.

Saturday, August 25, 1990

The negotiations broke down. When the talks opened for the day, both sides were optimistic that the process would move quickly toward a just conclusion. But it quickly became clear that each side had a different idea of what that conclusion would be.

The Mohawk argued that the military must pull back and police must leave the area entirely before the native barricades could come down. The government negotiators said the Mohawk would have to be the first ones to lay down their weapons.

The two sides also were far apart on the issue of immunity for the Mohawk. Mohawk negotiators said the Warriors could not be asked to simply surrender and rely on the good will of the police and the courts. The government team said there could be no amnesty and the Warriors would receive nothing more than assurances that they would be treated fairly under Canadian law.

Evacuation from Kahnawake

Monday, August 27, 1990

Premier Robert Bourassa called off all negotiations with the Mohawk. Then he ordered the Canadian Forces to dismantle the Mohawk barricades.

He accused the Mohawk of bargaining in bad faith. There was no reason, he said, to continue the negotiations. And he was not prepared to allow the standoff to continue indefinitely.

"We Québecers and Canadians cannot tolerate groups of citizens living in Québec choosing which laws they want to respect and which they want to ignore."

But the Mohawk said it was the government that was refusing to negotiate. And they warned that failure to find a peaceful settlement would lead to a bloodbath at the barricades.

"We're defending our homes and families. What we're doing is right," said Kahnawake chief Billy Two Rivers.

The Mohawk were backed up by the International Federation of Human Rights. A member of the federation's observer team at Oka said that the Mohawk had negotiated in good faith right from the start but the government was refusing to address the main issues in the dispute.

The military said it would carry out its orders to dismantle the barricades. But it did not say when the soldiers would move.

The chief of the defense staff, General John de Chastelain, said he hoped there would be no violence. His soldiers would, however, fire if fired upon.

"We cannot fail," he said, "because we are all that is left."

On the Mohawk side of the lines, the Warriors said they would not back down in the face of overwhelming odds. They might lose, they said, but they would inflict heavy casualties on their attackers.

Many Mohawk men, women and children decided to flee Kanesatake and Kahnawake before the army invasion. Others said they wanted no part of the violence but did not want to leave Mohawk land. They would stay in the settlements and hope for the best.

Tuesday, August 28, 1990

The Canadian Forces made their final preparations for the assault on the Mohawk barricades. Lieutenant-General Kent Foster announced that three Leopard assault tanks would be used to crush the barriers. He said the West German-built tanks would offer the best protection to his soldiers as they advanced on the Mohawk positions.

Tactical commander Brigadier-General Armand Roy was given the green light to attack at any time. General Foster advised people living near the barricades to take cover in their basements once the advance began.

The General said "unconditional surrender" was the only option for the Warriors.

Inside Kanesatake and Kahnawake, the Mohawk were preparing for war. Stretchers and bodybags were brought forward. Ashes were sprinkled on the Warriors and on the barricades. Last minute appeals for international intervention were made by the Mohawk Nation Office.

A convoy of more than 100 Mohawk – women, children, the sick and the elderly – left Kahnawake by car across the Mercier Bridge. Arrangements had been made in advance with the military and the police. But when

Lt.-General Kent Foster

(Canadian Forces photo)

the convoy reached the Montréal side of the bridge, the Mohawk found hundreds of angry whites lining the road. There were not enough police officers to control the crowd. The convoy moved forward. Hundreds of rocks were thrown at the cars. Several Mohawk were wounded. Many wept in terror long after the cars had passed through the crowd.

SQ searches Mohawk convoy as rock-throwers gather in distance

But there was one hopeful sign. Secret talks between the army and the Mohawk were going well. And it now appeared possible that a deal to reopen the Mercier Bridge and bring down the barricades at Kahnawake could be reached in time to prevent bloodshed.

That night, just after dusk, small planes began landing at an airstrip the Mohawk had built at Kahnawake. The planes came in just above the trees. By flying so low they were able to evade radar detection. They did not stay. Within a period of 75 minutes, 15 take-off and landings were recorded by the armed forces. The authorities did not have enough time to assess the situation and react. With no way of knowing for certain who was on board, they could not risk ordering the military to shoot down the planes.

But as they learned soon after, the cargo flown out on board the planes was made up of Warriors and their weapons heading for freedom. At least some of the planes turned south. Again flying just above the trees, they crossed the frontier into the United States at Rouses Point, New York where they were spotted by a U.S. Customs agent. Then the planes disappeared.

Wednesday, August 29, 1990

At dawn, columns of APCs arrived at the Kahnawake barricades. It was to be the day the issue would be decided one way or the other – at least as far as Kahnawake was concerned. Peace talks between the Mohawk and the army were taking place. Both sides were working hard to hammer out an agreement they knew would have to come within hours if violence was to be averted.

At the Farnham military base in the Eastern Townships, more troops and APCs were preparing to leave for Kahnawake. The three Leopard tanks were being loaded on to flatbed trucks. At 9:00 a.m., a call came from the army negotiators. The talks were progressing well, they said, and the convoy should remain in Farnham for the moment. There might not be any need for the tanks and armored vehicles.

It was a warm, sunny day. Crowds gathered on the army side of the barricades. Men brought their wives and children. Bikers showed up. Vigilante-types patrolled the crowd threatening to beat up photographers and members of the English-language press. There was a carnival atmosphere.

Angus Jacobs — A Police Interogation

Angus Jacobs, 47, is a stone mason and a Mohawk Indian from Kanesatake. He has lived there all his life. On Wednesday, the 26th of August, he was fed up with the absence of fresh food inside the Oka barricades. Since July 11th they had been manned on one side by Warriors and on the other by the Sûreté du Québec and then the Canadian army. With his girlfriend, he decided to drive north out of the village to buy food in Montréal. At the first road block he was stopped by soldiers and arrested by the Sûreté du Québec after showing identification. Six-and-a-half-hours later, he was permitted to make a phone call from a Montréal jail. This is his account of what happened during those six-and-a-half-hours.

"Around 11:30 in the morning we drove to the north barricade on St. Germain. We were going to buy food in Montréal. The army stopped us and SQ cops took our identification and when they came back they dragged me out of the car and shoved me into the back of a cruiser. They drove from the barricade and a cop grabbed me by the hair and pushed me to the floor.

"After driving around for fifteen minutes, they transferred me to a MUC police car and again they shoved my face into the floor so I couldn't see where I was going.

"We stopped at a building in the woods that I think was their headquarters. They showed me a photo of a masked man in the pine woods holding a gun. I think it was taken on July 11th. They said they knew it was me. I denied it. They called me a dirty Indian bastard. They put a shotgun in my ear and made me crawl on the floor and called me a dog and said that they were going to kill me like a dog if I didn't make a confession. For the next two-and-a-half-hours they took turns beating me. They split up into teams of two or three. They took off their heavy

shoes and put on sneakers so the marks wouldn't show as bad. They punched and kicked every part of my head and body. Not hard enough so I would be punched out but just on the border all the time. One of them grabbed me by the balls and twisted and then I almost passed out. Twice they put a gun to the side of my head and said that they were going to blow my brains out. I told them to go ahead and get it over with if that was what they were going to do, and who the hell was stopping them, not me. The beating kept up and I was hurting bad. By then my ears were running blood from being slapped over and over. I couldn't hear anything. My kidneys and stomach hurt real bad and my private parts were painful too. They kept saying I had to sign this confession they put in front of me. Finally I signed it just so they would stop. I didn't even look at what I signed. Then they took me downtown, and shoved me in a cell.

"Through it all I kept asking if I could phone my friend so she could get a lawyer for me. They just laughed and said no one could help me where they had me and there would be no fucking phone calls till I signed. They didn't let me make a call until I had been in custody for six-and-a-half-hours — by then it was about six o'clock. They never even read me my rights."

Angus Jacobs was charged with possession of a dangerous weapon and released on bail.

On the other side of the barricades, the Mohawk Warriors kept their heads down. They were waiting for the military assault.

By early afternoon, the peace talks had failed to produce an agreement. From his headquarters near Kahnawake, Lt.-Col. Greg Mitchell of the RCRs called for the convoy to roll out of Farnham. The armored vehicles were formed into a long line. Motors rumbling, the APCs, jeeps and trucks moved through the main gates of the base. They turned right and headed west down Highway 104 toward Kahnawake. Some of the APCs were tracked vehicles that are steered by levers in the same manner as bulldozers. Keeping them on the road is difficult. As a result, the convoy could move no faster than 50 kilometers per hour.

At 5:00 p.m., the military was ready to move. But as the soldiers stood waiting for the order, a small group of Mohawk Warriors emerged from

behind their barricade. The Mohawk were unarmed. They walked forward a few steps. Then, one placed an object on the road before him. It was a peace pipe. An army officer led a group of soldiers forward to meet the Mohawk. For a few minutes, they stood there talking. And they shook hands. The standoff at Kahnawake was over.

Minutes after the handshake, a Mohawk bulldozer began tearing down the barricades and filling in the trenches that had been dug to stop the tanks and APCs. A joint announcement said the Mohawk and the military would work together to tear down all the barricades and to reopen the Mercier Bridge. But the military warned that the job of repairing the roads and checking the bridge for damage and booby traps would take longer than just a couple of days.

For the Mohawk at Kanesatake, the news that the barricades were coming down at Kahnawake offered no reason to cheer. Now they were isolated. But it was fitting, said one Mohawk, that the drama would end where it began – at Kanesatake.

Peace talks between the government and the Mohawk were continuing at Dorval. The land dispute that sparked the standoff had long been resolved in principle and only the technical details on how the land would be bought by Ottawa and handed over to the Mohawk remained to be worked out. What defied resolution was the issue of what would become of the Mohawk who surrendered. They wanted guarantees that they would not become victims of revenge at the hands of the Sûreté du Québec. The Québec government said there could be no guarantee other than a promise of fair treatment under the law.

Thursday, August 30, 1990   Again, Premier Robert Bourassa called off the peace talks. This time, the reason was the decision by representatives of the moderate and traditionalist Six Nations Iroquois Confederacy to withdraw from the Mohawk negotiating team. The Confederacy team said it was getting out because it did not agree with some of the Warriors' demands and therefore could not negotiate in good faith.

Some of the members of the Kanesatake negotiating team were also critical of the Warriors for making demands which, they said, everyone

Quebec Premier Robert Bourassa

knew would never be accepted and which had little to do with the main issues surrounding the standoff. But they also condemned the Québec authorities for breaking off negotiations at a time when it appeared the two sides were close to an agreement.

At Kahnawake, Mohawk and soldiers continued the job of removing the barricades and making the roads passable. However, Chief Joe Norton accused the police of breaking the peace agreement by refusing to allow the free passage of food and medicine on to the reserve. Fellow chief Billy Two Rivers said the Mohawk could close off the Mercier Bridge even before it reopened. The police denied that they were preventing any supplies from reaching Kahnawake.

Friday, August 31, 1990

The negotiators for the Six Nations Iroquois Confederacy said the breakdown of the peace talks had nothing to do with them. And they were furious with the Québec government for breaking off the talks and then blaming it on the Confederacy.

"Our mandate was to get the parties back together so that this could be resolved," said negotiator Harvey Longboat. "We did that and came home."

Québec officials stuck to the position that without the moderate Confederacy, there would be little hope of making progress. The talks remained suspended although Mohawk negotiators gathered to bicker among themselves over who truly represented the Mohawk people.

Tom Siddon, the federal minister of Indian Affairs, announced that Ottawa had just about completed the process of acquiring the disputed land at Kanesatake in order to turn it over to the Mohawk.

"I have directed my officials to begin exploratory discussions with various people from Kanesatake with a view to start formal negotiations as soon as the barricades come down," he said.

The barricades at Kanesatake remained in place. But there were few Warriors left to hold them. Most of the Warriors had slipped away leaving only a small group of armed men to defend the community. And although the army remained on its side of the barricades, there were no Mohawk manning the northern or western perimeters of their land.

At Kahnawake, the Mohawk and the military continued the work of removing barricades and filling in trenches.

Saturday, Sept. 1, 1990

In the early morning, Kanesatake chief Francis Jacobs and his son Corey were badly beaten in their home by a group of Warriors. Chief Jacobs had criticized some Warriors for breaking into the home of a veterinarian who had left the community during the crisis. The home had been ransacked and vandalized.

Canadian Forces officials said the beating was a sign that all order had broken down in Kanesatake and that the lives of everyone inside the Mohawk-held territory were in danger. It was a situation, they said, that could not be tolerated.

At one p.m., the military moved against the Mohawk at Kanesatake. Soldiers in camouflage gear, their faces painted dark green, climbed over the undefended barricades along the northern, eastern and western perimeters and made their way into the pines. They were backed by APCs. Helicopters flew overhead.

Warrior known as "Lasagna" aims arrow

Warriors in commandeered golf cart on Highway 344 near burial gr
(Baxendale photo)

isagna'' gestures to army

Soldier/Warrior confrontations were frequent

Louis Hall — Return to the Longhouse

"There has been a 300-year dark age for the Great Law of Peace. It was used freely in the writing of the constitution of the United States of America but there is little knowledge of it among non-natives. Even among the Iroquois nations the Great Law of Peace was almost lost because of suppression by the white man's church and government. The chiefs who were teaching it had to go into hiding. The white man has always tried to eliminate the Longhouse law and replace it with his Indian Act."

"It was a Jewish lawyer who made me understand the importance of our traditional ways. I met this man during the negotiations for compensation for the land taken from us to build the St. Lawrence Seaway. He was a good lawyer too. In some cases he got us three times more for the land than the government offered. One day he asked me: 'What is the national religion of the Mohawk?'. I said 'The Longhouse'. 'How many in the Caughanawaga (Kahnawake) reserve practice it?' I exaggerated and said 'About half of the village.' He said 'Get the other half in. A national religion will help you. Indians all over North America should return to their traditional religion.' Then he said: 'Not all Jews are religious but they profess to a common religion. It is a force for unity and without it we could never have survived the persecution over the centuries.'

"This made sense to me because no race had been more persecuted than mine. So with a friend, Stanley Mayo, I started

to attend the Longhouse ceremonies. I think the next one was to be the 'first fruits of the season' ceremony, the Strawberry Festival.

"There was a pretty simple ceremony, not too heavy on the religious side, and when they danced, it was more fun than being in church. So I learned to enjoy traditional dances like the Great Feather Dance and the Creator's Dance. The next festival was at midsummer for the the first vegetable to ripen, the bean. Then came the corn festival in late August followed by October's harvest thanksgiving. The midwinter festival comes in January to celebrate the start of a new year. I attended them all that year.

"I had been brought up a Catholic but I slowly came to realize that was not the way my ancestors worshipped the Creator, so I converted. Now in 1990, the Longhouse membership is growing steadily and I think more will come to it after this crazy summer (of 1990)."

One column of soldiers moved slowly down the narrow dirt road toward the rear of the original barricade where on July 11 the Mohawk first clashed with the police. There, they were met by an unarmed, masked Warrior in one of the electric golf carts commandeered from the local golf course. The column stopped while the Warrior known as Bolt Pin shouted and swore at the soldiers. An officer gave the order to keep moving, and the lead APC rolled forward at a snail's pace. The Warrior refused to move. The APC bumped him on the chest pushing him backwards no more than a meter. Still, Bolt Pin refused to give ground. The driver of the APC switched off the motor.

While Bolt Pin was staring down the column, a dozen Warriors were being brought up to the line in the bucket of a front-end loader. They spread out, taking cover in the forest. Finally, Bolt Pin turned and headed back toward the Mohawk line. The soldiers resumed their slow march down the dirt road. When they reached the Mohawk line, they were again met by Warriors refusing to retreat. Soldiers on the flank of the column kneeled, and with fingers on the triggers of their C-7 assault rifles, they took aim at the Warriors. The Mohawk shouted insults at the soldiers, challenging them to fight it out with fists or guns.

The Warriors had sworn not to fire the first shot. One loudly begged for permission to "slug that fucking arrogant asshole" officer who was leading the soldiers. Another Warrior, hidden in the nearby foliage, screamed at the soldiers to fire. The soldiers maintained their discipline.

At that moment, Jennie Jack drove up on a four-wheel All-Terrain Vehicle. The British Columbia Indian had come to Kanesatake to act as an adviser and supporter to the Mohawk. She ordered the Warriors to move back. They were taken by surprise. When one didn't respond quickly enough to her order, she threatened to "kick your fuckin' ass."

Jennie Jack faces the army

Message to SQ on concrete block: They came, they saw, they ran.

Lasagna and soldier

The Warrior hidden in the foliage was becoming increasingly hysterical.

"C'mon. Shoot, you fuckers. Shoot," he screamed at the soldiers.

Jack went into the bushes herself and dragged him out.

The Warriors withdrew further down the dirt road. Negotiations were held. The military said its orders were to move to Highway 344 and tear down the Mohawk barricades on the two-lane highway. Squeezed in on three sides by the army advance, the Warriors and their supporters would be forced to withdraw into an area 200 meters by 100 meters bordering the Ottawa River. Within the area is an alcohol and drug abuse treatment center. It would become the headquarters for the Mohawk last stand.

After conferring among themselves, the Warriors agreed to retreat. Without a shot being fired, the Mohawk gave up the barricades they had built 54 days earlier when they turned back the Sûreté du Québec assault team.

There were now just two dozen armed Warriors left to hold off the Canadian Forces.

At Kahnawake, the final barricades on the Mercier Bridge were removed and the job of checking the bridge for structural damage or booby traps was proceeding on schedule.

At Oka the tension remained high through the night. At ten p.m., a shot rang out. Reporters said there was no doubt the shot had come from the army side of the line. Warriors sitting by the edge of the road near the entrance to the treatment center insisted the shot had kicked up dirt near them. Warrior Mad Jap and the Mohawks' legal adviser Stanley Cohen confronted the army commander. "You fired the first shot!" they said. "Don't you know there are women and children back there?"

The army denied the shot had been fired by a soldier. But one reporter said that soon after the shot had sounded she had seen a soldier being removed from the front line as an NCO (noncommissioned officer) berated him.

Most of the Warriors were back in the treatment center, or the TC as they called it, with their supporters. They took turns guarding the entrance to the TC where they sat on lawn chairs, AK-47s across their laps, chatting with a half-dozen reporters. The area was illuminated by high-powered search lights from across the road where Charlie Company of the Royal 22nd Regiment was on full stand-to. Dug in behind sandbags or atop APC Grizzlies, the soldiers held their .50 calibre machine guns, and C7 and C8 assault rifles. The occasional swoosh of parachute flares accented the sound of the helicopter blades beating overhead. A cacophony of eerie war whoops amplified through the Mohawk loudspeakers filled the air.

Inside the TC, the Mohawk welcomed as many reporters as they could accomodate, offering sandwiches, coffee and a chance to watch the 11 o'clock TV news. For most of the journalists, it would be their last time inside the TC.

Baxendale photo

Private Cloutier — Soldier

It was the stare seen around the world. And it made Private Patrick Cloutier a celebrity.

On September first, the Royal 22nd Regiment – the Vandoos – moved against the Mohawk barricades at Oka. With only a handful of Warriors left to face the army, the Mohawk withdrew without a fight. But as the soldiers moved forward, the Warriors confronted them at each point along the way.

When the army began setting up their razor wire fences near the site of the original barricade in the Pines, the Warrior known as Lasagna picked Pte. Cloutier as his target. The Mohawk walked up to the slightly-built, 20-year-old soldier. For a moment, Cloutier wavered, unsure what to do. When no orders came from his officer, Cloutier stuck out his chest and stared back at Lasagna. The two men were standing literally nose-to-nose.

Lasagna said, "Boo!"

Cloutier didn't flinch.

The Warrior called the private a "motherfucker" and asked him if he was ready to die. Cloutier never blinked. Lasagna continued to try to stare him down. Cloutier steadfastly returned the stare.

Eventually, it was Lasagna who turned away.

But the confrontation had been recorded by the cameras. And the image of the baby-faced soldier staring impassively into the eyes of the

fearsome Warrior appeared in newspapers, magazines and TV newscasts around the globe.

It was an image of bravery and discipline that the military hierarchy loved. Within days, Cloutier had been sent back to his military base in Québec City to begin a special course that would prepare him for a rapid promotion to the rank of master corporal.

Some of his fellow soldiers, however, said Cloutier's bravado was no big deal.

Much of Cloutier's 20 months in the Canadian Forces had been spent as a member of the Red Guard. The guards are the sentries who stand expressionless outside the Citadel, one of Québec City's most popular tourist sites. The sentries are constantly teased and provoked by tourists who want to pry some sort of facial reaction or movement from the stone-like soldiers.

The tourists tell jokes or pretend to toss things at the guards. Sometimes, girls will stand directly in front of a young guard and hike up their skirts or lift their blouses.

And that, said the other soldiers, is a lot tougher to deal with than Lasagna's taunts.

The barricade comes down

Sunday, Sept. 2, 1990

Vandoos fold Vietnam Vets flag

Checking for booby traps

At 8.30 a.m., the army moved their razor wire fences several meters forward. That brought the soldiers right up to the edge of the highway and to the perimeter of the Mohawk cemetery. The move was in preparation for the dismantling of the last barricade.

"It's just a pile of dirt," said Blackjack of the barricade he and his fellow Warriors had given up to the army.

But the Warriors said they had no plans to lay down their arms and surrender. Instead, they prepared for battle. They dug trenches and bunkers in the forest and across the mouth of the dirt road leading to the treatment center. There were 30 Mohawk women and children at the TC. And they helped in the preparations by burning tobacco and sweetgrass, the ashes of which were sprinkled on the Warriors and on the soldiers standing guard around the compound.

It had become a test of nerves. But it was a test the Mohawk could not win. The soldiers were more numerous, better disciplined and, more importantly, they worked in shifts. It was the military's strategy to keep the Mohawk on edge at all times. The Warriors were forced to be on guard 24 hours a day.

It became too much for one Warrior, a Micmac from Cape Breton known as the General. He accosted an army officer along the line.

"We're getting tired of waiting," he said. "Do you plan to kill us all in here? I want to know now. If you're going to kill us all, do it now."

The officer remained impassive.

"I have nothing to say, sir," he replied.

In the early afternoon Jennie Jack, climbed on her all-terrain vehicle and drove out from the TC to where the journalists were gathered on Highway 344. She carried a list with her. On the list were the names of a dozen or so broadcast and print media the Mohawk had chosen to be with them during their final stand. Her announcement was greeted by protests from those not on the list. But there were no complaints from those who were invited to remain. They were plainly delighted by the turn of events. Later some critics would accuse the Mohawk of attempting to manipulate press coverage of the crisis by rewarding only those reporters who wrote positive things about the Mohawk. They pointed to the glaring omission of Montréal's major English language daily, *the Gazette* from the list.

Further down the road, the army was beginning the task of dismantling the main barricade. First, a team of combat engineers carefully checked the barricade for booby traps. They found none. Then a soldier lowered the Vietnam Veteran's flag, which the Warriors had left flying above the barricade. In a show of respect, the soldiers carefully folded the flag and handed it over to a Mohawk Warrior and a legal adviser.

The demolition squad and a single army bulldozer began clearing away the barricade. Although it had been constructed of huge pine trees, two SQ squad cars and other smashed vehicles as well as tons of bulldozed dirt, it took the army only 15 minutes to complete the job. For the first time since July 11, there was an unobstructed view from the "Hill of Sand" along Highway 344 and down into the village of Oka.

The soldiers were now content to simply hold their positions. Military spokesmen insisted that they had no timetable and the army was willing to allow the standoff to drag on indefinitely now that the barricades had come down. Unless the Warriors surrendered, it would be the military who dictated when the confrontation would end.

Monday, Sept. 3, 1990

Army wire closes in on Warriors at TC

In the early morning, the army moved its razor wire across Highway 344 and up to the Mohawk front line. A shot was fired from the army side. No one was wounded. But the Warriors scrambled into their trenches in preparation for an army assault. The 53-year-old Warrior known as Mad Jap charged to the front. Unarmed and wearing no mask or military clothing, he marched back and forth between the soldiers and the Warriors.

"Hold your fire," he shouted to his fellow Warriors. "They're trying to provoke you into this."

He called on the military to send forward an officer for negotiations. Again, the confrontation ended without bloodshed but with the Mohawk pushed farther back. There was no longer any hope of escape. They were surrounded on three sides by hundreds of soldiers behind razor wire fences. On the fourth side was a steep hill leading down to the Ottawa River. Soldiers patrolled the shoreline.

Although the situation had become desperate for the Mohawk, they remained steadfast in their refusal to surrender. There was little left to gain, but the Warriors said they would rather fight and die than surrender and be handed over to the Sûreté du Québec. Some Mohawk who had fallen into the hands of the police during the crisis said they had been beaten and tortured. The police strongly denied the accusations. But the Warriors believed the stories. And their fears only grew when the police paraded their paddy wagons around Kanesatake after the army had moved in. The Mohawk took that display as a "we're going to get you" message.

Inside the TC, the Warriors continued to prepare for a battle they knew they could not win. For some, there were quiet moments with their wives and children. These would, perhaps, be the final such moments. There were hugs and kisses. And then the Warriors picked up their weapons and marched into the forest to take up their positions near the razor wire.

At Kahnawake, soldiers surrounded the site of the traditional Mohawk government, the Longhouse. Police then moved in and searched the building. They seized dozens of weapons, although the Mohawk claimed the arms had been planted in the building by the security forces. Some 30 women were inside the Longhouse when the raid began. They rushed out and began shouting and shoving the soldiers. Two of the women were injured in the scuffle. Earlier in the day, Mohawk women and children at the Mercier Bridge had also fought with soldiers.

The office of Québec's chief coroner announced that an autopsy had been ordered on the body of an elderly Mohawk. Joe Armstrong had died in hospital of heart failure the previous day. He had been among the 200 Mohawk who were attacked by rock-throwing protesters while driving off the Mercier Bridge the previous week. The Mohawk believed the World War Two veteran died as a result of the terrifying experience at the bridge.

Jennie Jack — An Education

Jennie Jack is 35, a Tlinkit Indian from British Columbia where she is a third year law student at University of British Columbia. She came to Kanesatake 10 days after the crisis erupted to support the Mohawk. She is the mother of two children.

On Sunday September 2nd, Jennie was acting as a press liason. It was she who announced to the more than one hundred media people assembled, that the Mohawk would permit a picked handful to join them in the treatment center:

"The army wants to cut you off from us, we want you to witness what they do to us because none of us will be around to tell the story," she said.

At that time the army was slowly squeezing down the perimeters, systematically reducing the Warriors' territory. It was felt by the Mohawk that there would be a fight to the finish and that the Warriors were ready to sacrifice their lives but would give a good account of themselves in so doing.

"I knew what I was getting into when I came and we all knew it would come to this. The boys have already been tortured so that's not much to look forward to. We would rather be shot by a bullet than that."

Reflecting on her soon to be wasted education: "It blows me away to think I did four years of political science and three years of law school. The idea was to learn how to run a country and how civilized governments work. Then I come here to witness three levels of Canadian government in action. What a joke."

Tuesday, Sept. 4, 1990

The army put on display the weapons allegedly seized from the Kahnawake Longhouse. Among the asault rifles and ammunition clips was a .50 caliber tripod-mounted machine gun. Its bullets can pierce the armor of an APC at a range of more than one kilometer. Mohawk chief Joe Norton continued to insist that there had been no weapons in the Longhouse before the police and army arrived.

Military officials pronounced the Mercier Bridge to be safe but said the bridge could not be opened to the public until the access roads had been secured by the soldiers.

At Oka, Mayor Jean Ouellette called for a round-the-clock police presence once the standoff would be over. He said the people of Oka wanted to know they would be protected from the Warriors. And he rejected Mohawk suggestions that native peacekeepers be given a role in policing the community.

In Ontario, five Hydro Ontario towers were brought down on the Chippewa of the Thames Indian reserve near London. The towers fell in the middle of the night after bolts were removed from the base of the 40-meter structures. Mohawk sympathizers were believed to be responsible.

Wednesday, Sept. 5, 1990

Federal Indian Affairs minister Tom Siddon met with chiefs from the Six Nation Confederacy and other native leaders in Ottawa. They told him the Warriors at the Kanesatake treatment center were under severe stress from the military. And they said that situation could only harm efforts to bring about a peaceful end to the standoff.

While things were relatively quiet during the day, at night the military would step up its campaign to intimidate the Mohawk. Soldiers would shout insults at the Warriors and the women. They would shine powerful spotlights and throw flares into the Warrior-held compound while helicopters hovered just above the trees. The Warriors would shout their own insults and shine their own lights back at the soldiers. But the constant night games left the Warriors lacking in sleep. The chiefs asked Mr. Siddon to order an end to the army tactics. He replied only that he would pass on the request to the military as soon as possible.

That evening, the military announced that the access roads through Kahnawake to the Mercier Bridge had been secured. The bridge would reopen to the public at six a.m. the next morning.

SQ on Montréal side of bridge

Thursday, Sept. 6, 1990

The Mercier Bridge reopened. Long lines of cars were strung out in the morning fog along the main roads leading into Kahnawake. At six a.m., the army gave the signal to proceed. The drivers honked and waved to the television cameras filming the event for the evening news.

With the opening of the bridge and the access roads, residents of Chateauguay and the neighboring suburbs along the south shore of the St. Lawrence no longer had to make a long, time-consuming and traffic-ridden detour to reach the island of Montréal. The blockade of the Mercier Bridge had been the cause of many violent anti-Mohawk demonstrations during the standoff.

But the end of the blockade did not mean relations between the Mohawk and their white neighbors were back to normal.

Freighter passes through St. Lawrence Seaway at Kahnawake

"They're afraid of us," said one Mohawk. "You can see it in their eyes when they drive through the reserve."

At Kanesatake, the Warriors and the soldiers continued their standoff. The chief of the Canadian Forces defense staff, General John de Chastelain, offered the Warriors a deal. They could lay down their weapons and give themselves up to the army. Rather than be handed over to the provincial police, they would be taken to the Canadian Forces base at Farnham, Québec where they would be held while police investigated their actions and decided whether to press charges. The Warriors turned down the offer.

Friday, Sept. 7, 1990

Premier Robert Bourassa again called on the two dozen Warriors holding out at Kanesatake to surrender to the armed forces. He said there could be no other terms offered by his government.

The Warriors are criminals who must eventually be brought to justice, he said. And he urged Canada's native leaders to disown the Warriors and to put pressure on them to lay down their arms.

"If they want to keep their support," he said of the native leaders, "I don't think they should associate with people related to criminal acts."

The Warriors responded with a peace offer of their own. They said the standoff could end peacefully if the military pulled back and allowed the Warriors to leave the treatment center without fear of arrest. As well, they asked that the Sûreté du Québec be withdrawn from Oka.

The offer was rejected by the military and the Québec government.

Saturday, Sept. 8, 1990

A four-man army patrol slipped through the razor wire at Kanesatake just after 4 a.m. They were scouting the Mohawk defenses in the forest when

they stumbled upon a Warrior asleep in his trench. It was Randy Horne, the ironworker who goes by the name of Spudwrench. He woke up as soon as the soldiers touched him. In the struggle, he was able to reach his knife. He stabbed at his attackers, wounding two of them. But he was quickly overwhelmed and badly beaten. Hearing Spudwrench shout, other Warriors came running. The soldiers fled into the darkness and back across their lines.

Spudwrench was taken to the treatment center where a doctor examined him and said the Warrior could be suffering from a fractured skull. He had to be taken to hospital. An ambulance was brought up to the razor wire and the wounded Mohawk was taken to the Montréal General Hospital where doctors treated what turned out to be minor head injuries.

For Spudwrench, the conflict was over.

Sunday, Sept. 9, 1990

Doxator, faithkeeper Bruce Elijah, Antone arrive at TC

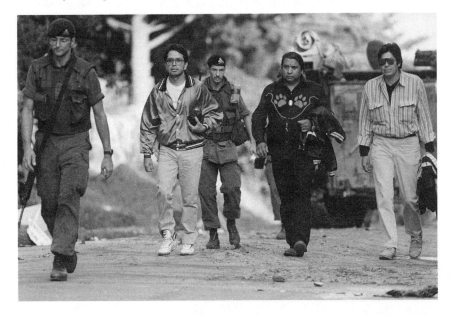

The military announced there would be no more reconnaissance missions on the Mohawk side of the lines. Major John Paul MacDonald said Spudwrench was being held under "military protection" in hospital and would be taken to a military base once doctors declared him well enough to leave.

At the barricades in Oka, C company was replaced by A company. There were rumours that the move was ordered because C company and its commander, Major Alain Tremblay, had become too aggressive in their dealings with the Warriors. But military officials said the change was a routine rotation designed to keep fresh troops on the barricades.

The Warriors got a new negotiator. Oneida chief Bob Antone arrived at the treatment center to try hammer out a "disengagement" agreement. One of the proposals he put forward called for the Warriors to surrender and be held at a military base outside Québec. However, there was no sign from either side that the proposal would be accepted.

In Vancouver, federal Justice minister Kim Campbell said Ottawa would not negotiate any amnesty or immunity for the Warriors. Their only option, she insisted, was to surrender to the armed forces.

"The Warriors do not represent legitimate native grievances legitimately advanced. They carry guns. They are resisting enforcement of the law and we will not negotiate with them."

Monday, Sept. 10, 1990

American lawyer Stanley Cohen

The military announced that Spudwrench had been released from hospital and, along with his wife, had voluntarily agreed to be placed under military custody. The couple were taken to the Canadian Forces Base at Farnham.

Inside the treatment center at Kanesatake, the Warriors' legal adviser spent the day working on a new proposal to end the standoff. Lawyer Stanley Cohen of the U.S. described the plan as "significantly different" from the Mohawk previous offers. It would be presented to the army the next day, he said.

At Kahnawake, the army arrested two members of the reserve's police force and handed them over to the Sûreté du Québec. Chief peacekeeper Joseph Montour and his assistant-chief, Warren White, had left the reserve to pick up a police car from a nearby garage. When they returned, soldiers guarding the entrance to Kahnawake noticed that both men were wearing their police sidearms. They were charged with possession of dangerous weapons and later released on the promise they would appear in court at a later date.

Johnny Cree — Our Land

Johnny Cree is a faithkeeper of the Longhouse: "There are only a few of us. It's something that just comes upon us. The ceremonies and teachings are passed on by elders. It's a lifetime job." He tells a story to illustrate some of the Longhouse beliefs:

"When I was a little boy an elder asked me who is the Creator's father. I said I didn't know. Then he asked if I knew the story of creation. Again my answer was no. So he said he would tell it to me:

"There was a woman in the Sky World who became impregnated by the wind which had also uprooted a tree leaving a big hole. As the woman walked, she looked through the hole and saw the ocean, a land of water. She leaned over to take a better look, lost her balance and fell through. As she fell, she grasped out with both hands and in one hand she grabbed tobacco, the voice to our Creator, and in the other were strawberries, the heart of our Creator. As she fell, the birds spotted her and went underneath her to cushion her fall. As she floated down, a great turtle came out of the ocean but his shell was so hard the watching animals saw she would be hurt so they tried to go down to the bottom of the ocean to bring up mud to put on the back of the turtle to soften her fall. But none of them could do it except the muskrat who kept going down and back until he had covered the turtle with mud.

"That place became known as Turtle Island and it is North America. Soon she gave birth to a daughter and it came to pass that her daughter too was made pregnant by the wind. She gave birth to twins. One was the Creator and when he grew he set about the business of making the oceans and the mountains and streams and putting the trees in place. He was very serious. But the other was a joker and he ran

around making frivolous things like rapids. He was a practical joker too and when he saw his brother lying on the lake sleeping from all his work he pushed him. His brother then fell over what we now know as Niagara Falls.

"And the elder asked me again: 'Now do you know who the Creator's Father was?' I replied, 'No.' He said, 'What are the two things you cannot do without?' I thought a bit then said, 'Water and air.' 'Right. But which one is the Creator's Father?' I still didn't know. 'Then what is the first thing you need when born?' 'Air' I said . 'And what is the last thing you do before dying?' I said, 'Draw a last breath.' So I knew then that air was the Father of Creation.

"The story explains why Mother Earth is so important to us. She gives the land and the trees that breathe the oxygen that sustains all life on earth. Her breath is all over the world giving and sustaining life. Without Mother Earth and the trees, there would be no life.

"If you can understand the importance of what I have told you then you will begin to know what the Longhouse people are all about. We do not have a sense of ownership like the white man. We are the caretakers of the land for our children and future generations but we are responsible to Mother Earth to see that our children and their children will be able to walk the land and still see the green trees and grass and clear streams that give clean water and fresh air."

In Ottawa, federal Indian Affairs minister Tom Siddon met with native leaders from across Canada. The aim of the meeting was to exchange ideas on ending the crisis peacefully. Instead, the gathering produced only an exchange of insults. Mr. Siddon accused the native leaders of encouraging the Warriors to drag out the standoff. He said the chiefs should have condemned the Warriors' tactics right from the beginning. And he told the chiefs they were wasting their time when they asked for amnesty or special treatment for the Warriors.

The chiefs responded that Mr. Siddon was an insensitive fool who should resign.

Mr. Siddon said those kind of statements would do nothing to improve the situation.

Tuesday, Sept. 11, 1990

The Warriors presented their new peace proposal. Like the government's proposals, it called for them to surrender to the military. But instead of the police deciding on what charges would be laid against them, the Warriors' fate would be put in the hands of a special commission made up of natives and non-natives.

Within minutes of seeing the proposal, Premier Robert Bourassa rejected it as "unacceptable."

"There is no question of a special category of individuals receiving treatment under the law different from any other citizen of Québec," he said.

Wednesday, Sept. 12, 1990

Randy "Spudwrench" Horne became the first of the Kanesatake Warriors to be charged in court. Sûreté du Québec officers arrived at the Farnham military base in the early morning. They took Spudwrench and his wife, Stephany Hemlock Horne, to a court in the lower Laurentian town of St. Jerome. His face swollen from the injuries he had sustained four days earlier, Spudwrench showed no emotion as the charges were read out. There were five charges: wearing a disguise with the intent of committing a crime; mischief; obstructing justice; participating in a riot; and possession of a dangerous weapon. The last charge carries a maximum sentence of 10 years in prison. His lawyer asked that he be tried by judge and jury.

After the arraignment, the police drove the Hornes back to Farnham where they were again placed under military guard.

In Québec City, the provincial minister for Intergovernmental Affairs held out an olive branch. Gil Remillard described the Mohawk as a "great aboriginal people." And he said the Québec government was ready to recognize at least some degree of Mohawk autonomy. He also condemned efforts by some parents in Chateauguay to keep Mohawk children out of the local schools.

Thursday, Sept. 13, 1990

Provincial public security minister Sam Elkas telephoned Terry Doxtator, an Oneida acting as a negotiator for the Mohawk. He had an offer for the Warriors at Kanesatake.

Throw out the journalists still inside, he said. The military would move the journalists on the outside back from the barricades. A bus would be driven up to the front gate of the treatment center. The Warriors would board the bus and be taken to the Farnham military base.

"We would move in. No sign of surrender, per se. This way here, nobody would be seen, nobody would be humiliated in any way."

The Warriors said the offer was insulting and ridiculous. It's not a matter of saving face, they said. It's a matter of Mohawk rights.

The offer was rejected.

When asked by jounalists about the offer, Mr. Elkas denied the telephone conversation with Mr. Doxtator had ever taken place. But Mr. Doxtator had made a tape recording of the conversation, and he played it back for reporters.

At Kanesatake, the army tightened the screws a little bit more. The telephone lines into the treatment center were cut. And the soldiers began jamming shortwave and cellular telephone communications out of the TC.

Forces spokesman Major John Paul MacDonald said the lines had been cut to "encourage" the Warriors to use the "hot line" that ran directly to military headquarters. He said the military wanted to show the Warriors that it was "serious about conducting negotiations."

The new policy made it difficult for the small band of journalists inside the TC to file their stories. They said the army was ignoring the constitutional guarantees of freedom of the press.

The military told the journalists to get out of the TC.

"I strongly urge you to leave by nightfall," said Major George Rousseau.

The soldiers put up light towers to better illuminate the Mohawk side of the razor wire.

Friday, Sept. 14, 1990

The Warriors came under attack from an unexpected source. George Erasmus, the Grand Chief of the Assembly of First Nationas, said that by taking up arms against the authorities the Warriors were hurting the cause of native rights across Canada. He accused the federal and Québec governments of carrying out a smear campaign against the Mohawk. But he said the actions of the Warriors were making the job easier for the white authorities.

Saturday, Sept. 15, 1990

The Canadian Association of Journalists condemned the military for cutting communications between the journalists inside the TC and their newsrooms.

Association president Charles Bury said the action represented a "serious attack" against freedom of the press.

The army said Warriors had been using the reporters' cellular phone to make subversive calls. The reporters said that was not true.

Hundreds of Mohawk supporters – both native and non-native – from the United States and Canada arrived at Oka to show their solidarity with the Kanesatake band. But police prevented them from reaching the town itself.

Sunday, Sept. 16, 1990

Brigadier-General Armand Roy said the military was now in the "final stage of negotiations" with the Mohawk inside the treatment center.

"Political authorities are aware of what we are doing. They are not involved in these negotiations."

He also defended the military's decision to cut off telephone service between the TC and the outside world.

Chief Billy Two Rivers — Pro Wrestler to Public Servant

In the early days of the crisis, Billy Two Rivers' main concern was ensuring that the people of Kahnawake received adequate food and medical care despite the police blockade of the reserve.

Two Rivers was one of Kahnawake's most senior traditional chiefs and a member of the band council. And according to Mohawk tradition, chiefs are true public servants. They serve, rather than lead, the people.

The 55-year-old Two Rivers spent the first weeks of the standoff running food, medicine, and the sick across the St. Lawrence River between Kahnawake and Montréal on board his boat.

On July 26th, Two Rivers went to Ottawa to speak to the opposition Liberal Party's committee on aboriginal affairs. He made an eloquent plea for understanding and respect for the Mohawk cause. His ability to play to the cameras and the tape recorders with short, clear statements ensured that his words would be heard on TV and radio newscasts across Canada. And when he returned to Kahnawake, he took over as one of the Mohawk's chief negotiators and spokesmen.

He held the jobs until the barricades at Kahnawake came down. Then he shaved his head and went up to northern Québec to play a role in a Hollywood-style feature film on the first contacts between Indians and the missionaries sent by France to help colonize the new world.

Show business and public-speaking were nothing new for Two Rivers. When he was in his twenties, he travelled the world as a professional wrestler. His role was that of the fearsome but upright and kind-hearted champion who won most of his bouts against the villains. And it was that same role he played during the negotiations over the Mohawk crisis.

"I want to make sure that in this final stage of negotiations there is no distraction and we can conclude our mission professionally without again having to use military armaments," he said.

Military officials said talks over the "hot line" with the Warriors were going well and that the people inside the TC were getting all the food, medicine, and clothing they needed.

But the Warriors said shipments of warm clothing were not getting through even though the temperature was dropping to the freezing mark at night and the children were cold. Of the food that was reaching them, much of it had been pierced by army bayonets. And no medicine was being allowed through unless the Warriors made a specific request for the medication over the "hot line."

The Warriors began raiding the evacuated homes near the TC in search of the food and clothing they said they were being denied by the army blockade.

In Kahnawake, the Mohawk delivered "eviction notices" to the soldiers stationed on the reserve. They said the military had accomplished its mission of reopening the roads through Kahnawake and was now trespassing on Mohawk land. The military ignored the tactic.

Monday, Sept. 17, 1990

The Mohawk said negotiations with the military had reached an impasse despite statements by army officials that the talks were progressing well.

Bob Antone of the Six Nations Iroquois Confederacy said a peace agreement must include provisions for future negotiations on some form of Mohawk sovereignty. But he said the federal and provincial governments were refusing to talk with the Mohawk, and the army had no mandate to negotiate anything but the surrender of the Warriors.

A lawyer and representatives of the Canadian Association of Journalists and the Federation Professionelle des Journalistes du Québec were scheduled to meet with the reporters who still remained with the Mohawk inside the TC. They wanted to inform the reporters that they were under no obligation to submit to interrogation by the police or military if they left the compound.

The meeting was to be held at the main gate to the center. It never took place. At the last moment, the army cancelled the meeting without explanation.

The journalists and their association officials were furious. They accused the federal and provincial governments of behaving like dictatorships by allowing the army to flout the freedom of the press guarantees that are part of any democratic system.

Government representatives said it was all in the hands of the army.

Two newspapers – The Montréal Gazette and The Ottawa Citizen – announced that they would go to court in a bid to overturn the warrant under which the cellular telephone service inside the TC had been cut.

Tuesday, Sept. 18, 1990

The military and Québec police launched another raid on Kahnawake. They were looking for weapons which they believed the Mohawk had hidden on Tekakwitha Island – the site of Kahnawake's hospital and marina. The island is joined to the mainland by a short bridge at one end. But the soldiers and police moved in by boat and helicopter. At 2:30 p.m., they were dropped at the western end of the island and began moving slowly east toward the bridge. When word of the raid reached the Mohawk, they were enraged. Hundreds of men, women and children raced to the bridge to confront the soldiers.

There were only a few dozen soldiers there to meet the crowd. The police and the other soldiers were engaged in the search operation. They were far back sweeping the ground for weapons and raiding the marina for liquor.

ier carries balloon - part of device to deter helicopter landings

combat section with fixed bayonets guard TC compound

Warrior reflects as soldier and helicopter patrol Ottawa River at beach of TC compound

Warriors and friends gather for last time within the TC compound

Prayers to the Great Creator

Soldier observes from perch above the TC compo

Chief Joe Norton

Antone borrows press phone

Wednesday, Sept. 19, 1990

Kahnawake chief Joe Norton told the Mohawk to remain calm. But he was powerless to control their rage.

It began with shouts warning the army to leave Mohawk land. Rocks started to rain down on the soldiers. And then the Mohawk poured across the bridge to attack the soldiers with their fists. The soldiers dropped back. The Mohawk kept coming. They punched and kicked any soldiers they could reach. Tear gas was fired into the crowd. The Mohawk attempted to retreat but their path had been blocked by a truck parked on the bridge to prevent the army from crossing. Some jumped into the polluted river to escape the effects of the gas.

With nowhere to go, the Mohawk regrouped and charged into the army ranks again. One soldier was caught and dragged into the crowd where he was beaten into semi-consciousness. He was saved from worse injuries by a member of the local Mohawk police force, the Peacekeepers. Another soldier had half his ear ripped off. And 17 others would require medical treatment as a result of the confrontation.

(At the TC in Kanesatake, the holed-up Warriors were watching the battle on television. Each time a Mohawk was seen landing a punch, the building erupted in cheers. Not only did the Warriors enjoy watching the soldiers take a beating, but the sight of other Mohawk fighting with the army made them feel less isolated.)

The army gave as good as it got. Soldiers struck back with rifle butts. Seventy-five Mohawk were treated in hospital for exposure to tear gas, cuts and bruises, and in at least one case, broken bones. While the two sides fought, army helicopters rushed reinforcements to the battle site. The brawl came to an end when soldiers fired shots in the air while moving backward. The Mohawk did not retreat. But they stopped coming forward.

It was not until 9:00 p.m. that the army helicopters were able to airlift out the last of the soldiers.

Both sides defended their actions. The army said its job was to restore order and security in the area, and that meant separating the Mohawk from their weapons. They said the raid had turned up more than 50 weapons as well as beer and liquor that was being sold at the marina without license.

Mike, a spokesman for the Mohawk Nation Office, said the people had no choice but to fight back.

"They were invading our territory. We cannot accept any foreign forces on Mohawk territory, and we're going to continue to protest any future incursions," he said.

The army commander for Kahnawake, RCR Lieutenant-Colonel Greg Mitchell, said the raid would not be the last. But next time, he said, the soldiers would be given plexi-glass shields and riot helmets – and they would come in greater numbers.

There is nothing left to discuss, said the army in a letter to the Mohawk holding out at Kanesatake.

The Mohawk said they agreed.

"There is no point in talking with the military," said negotiator Bob Antone. "Their position has not changed and is not going to."

For two weeks, the two sides had passed each other proposals and letters across the razor wire. But the negotiations had made no progress.

The Mohawk said they would "disengage" if they received assurances that formal negotitatons on the issue of Mohawk rights would begin. But the military said it could not negotiate political issues. And it said the Warriors would be talking to no one but the military until the standoff came to an end. The standoff would end, said one army letter, one way or the other, with or without the Warriors' consent.

Thursday, Sept. 20, 1990

"The army's task is nearing completion," said Lieutenant-General Kent Foster. "We have removed the barricades and opened the public thoroughfares. What remains to be done is to complete the restoration of the normal conditions of public safety and security in the affected areas."

Although he added that the army had no plans to move against the Warriors inside the TC and Kanesatake, the Mohawk took the statement to mean the end was coming soon – at least as far as the military was concerned. Either the Warriors surrender to the army or it would withdraw from Kanesatake leaving the community under the control of the Sûreté du Québec.

Speaking for the Mohawk, Bob Antone said the statement amounted to an ultimatum. He accused the military and police of wanting to crush the spirit of the Mohawk people.

Military officials said it was not an ultimatum because there was no time limit. But they added that the army could not remain at Oka forever.

Friday, Sept. 21, 1990

The Kanesatake Mohawk Emergency Measures Committee agreed to the establishment of a police force that would include as many as 20 native officers to patrol the Oka-Kanesatake area.

The force would be under the control of the Sûreté du Québec, and none of the native officers would be Mohawk. But the committee said it had little choice.

"It's the best we can do in a bad situation," said spokesman Linda Simon.

The committee said the plan would "provide a level of comfort and security, along with an easing of tensions for the Mohawk of Kanesatake." It added that the agreement was in no way related to the negotiations over the fate of the Mohawk still holding out at the treatment center.

The plan did not receive an enthusiastic reception from some Mohawk. They argued that any plan which left the Sûreté du Québec in charge of police operations at Kanesatake could

Major John Paul MacDonald — "Doing our Job"

Major John Paul MacDonald, is director of Public Affairs of the Canadian Armed Forces, Québec Region. He was, with a staff of seven, responsible for liason with the press at Kanesatake from September 10th, when he replaced Major Richard Larouche, until the army left the area. Born in Montréal, Major MacDonald is 32, married with two children, a girl 3 and a boy 4. He is a graduate of McGill University. His name and face became familiar to Canadians from coast to coast throughout the last weeks of the siege at Oka.

MacDonald served as an infantry officer with the Royal 22nd Regiment prior to his posting to Public Affairs and spent three years with the Canadian contingent at Lahr, Germany. His father served in the Canadian army during the Second World War and his brother is in the Royal Canadian Navy. He says he is proud to serve in an army that is well disciplined and has a proven record of effective peace-keeping throughout the world.

"Our men's orders were not to retaliate to taunts and gestures from the Mohawk under any circumstances. Quite apart from the staring contests that everyone saw on television, the intimidation was pretty intense. When the men took food into the TC compound, they were called every name you could imagine and the women spat all over them. That isn't easy for anyone to take but no one buckled under the pressure. Yes, there were some lapses – when some of our men tried to steal the Mohawk warrior flag from the entrance to the TC center it might

have provoked retaliation and those responsible were removed from the front line and in some cases disciplined. The men were repeatedly reminded not to react to intimidation.

"For the most part I was impressed at the professionalism of the press and this operation should say something about the way we are in Canada. I can't think of any army in the world that would have kept the press so well informed. Obviously it caused some problems having the press so close to the action but we live in a democracy so we act accordingly. When we cut the phones and supplies to the reporters inside it was to concentrate attention on the negotiations via the hot line and we felt that was imperative.

"For an operation where the tension was present over such a long period there were very few injuries to army personnel. There were a few scratches and bruises the last day when the Warriors came out at Oka. The knife thrusts by "Spudwrench" to two men only cut through their clothing. At Kahnawake, one soldier was hit by a crowbar and had a fairly severe concussion. Another had part of an ear re-attached surgically after losing it during one of the weapon searches. Some of the men took kicks in the groin and a few punches but really nothing else worth mentioning.

"I doubt if anyone will be picked out for special recognition. We are more like the British at this kind of thing, that is we don't go in for 'fruit salad.' We did the job we are paid to do. Some may have their performance mentioned in their service record and senior command will probably congratulate all the men on a job well done and that will be it."

SQ director and Quebec public security minister

only lead to trouble between the Mohawk and the SQ. And some said the native officers would be looked upon as traitors who could expect even less cooperation from the Mohawk than could the regular SQ officers.

On the outskirts of Oka, police shut down the peace camp. The camp was set up on September 3rd by supporters of the Mohawk. At one point, as many as 700 people – natives and non-natives from across Canada – were staying at the camp. From the beginning, police put pressure on them to leave.

Just after six o'clock in the evening, the police told the 50 or so campers still remaining on the site to clear out or face arrest. All but a dozen left. At seven o'clock, the police moved in. They dragged away the protestors who refused to leave and tore down the tents and flags set up by the campers. Within a half-hour, the site was once again an empty field.

Saturday, Sept. 22, 1990

The director-general of the Sûreté du Québec, Robert Lavigne, arrived at Kanesatake for a tour with Canadian Forces Lieutenant-Colonel Pierre Daigle. The colonel showed the SQ leader the army positions and pointed out potential problems as far as policing Kanesatake was concerned. It was another sign that the army was serious in its promise to pull out of Kanesatake and allow the SQ to take over the job of patrolling the area.

Sunday, Sept. 23, 1990

Lt.-Col. Daigle

The Kanesatake Mohawk changed their minds about accepting a police force made up of native officers under the control of the Sûreté du Québec. After a long and heated debate, the emergency committee voted 22-18 to reject the plan.

Committee member Linda Simon said she was discouraged by the reversal. She said it would make it harder for Mohawk negotiators to convince the other side that they were able to speak or sign agreements on behalf of the Mohawk people.

The Mohawk rejection of the plan was not, however, binding on the Sûreté du Québec or the Québec government. The native officers could still be deployed at any time.

American civil rights activist Jesse Jackson arrived in Montréal to prepare a television documentary on the Mohawk crisis. He said he had come as a journalist. But he said he also wanted to find a peaceful end to the crisis.

"Hopefully, through dialogue and through the interviewing process, the tensions will ease and the bloodshed will stop," he said.

The military said it too hoped for an end to the confrontation but that Jackson would not be playing a part in the resolution. It said he would be treated like everyone else. And that meant he would not be allowed to cross the army lines or communicate with the Warriors at the treatment center.

Monday, Sept. 24, 1990

Cohen leaves TC

Jesse Jackson went to Kanesatake. Accompanied by Kahnawake chief Joe Norton, a camera crew, and half-a-dozen supporters, Rev. Jackson swept into the Kanesatake community center and food bank. It was more like the visit of campaigning politician than that of a journalist. The former candidate for the Democratic Party's 1988 presidential nomination shook hands, signed autographs, and even kissed babies.

But he didn't get into the treatment center to talk with the Mohawk involved in the siege. As promised, the military refused to allow him to cross army lines.

He did meet with the provincial minister of Native Affairs, John Ciaccia. Rev. Jackson told the minister that the crisis could be resolved if both sides worried more about avoiding violence and less about saving face.

Then, Rev. Jackson and his crew packed up and went back to the United States.

Inside the TC just after dark, two of the men decided to test the strength of the army's perimeter. The Mohawk negotiators at the TC had said that one way or another, the standoff would have to end within the next few days even if that meant laying down weapons and walking out. Some of the Warriors feared they would face long prison sentences. And they wanted to know how good were their chances of escaping. The two men found an unguarded spot along the line and passed through the razor wire. Soldiers quickly spotted the two and shone their powerful searchlights on the pair. The two men retreated back inside the compound.

The military feared an escape attempt was underway. Extra soldiers rushed out of camp. Some lined Highway 344. Others raced into the forest on either side of the compound in search of anyone attempting to breach the razor-wire defenses. They found no one.

Also that evening, the Warriors' American legal advisor picked up the telephone "hot line" and told the army that he would be coming out of the TC. Stanley Cohen asked that his lawyer be present when he left. The army agreed.

At 9:00 p.m., Mr. Cohen walked down the dirt road leading from the TC to Highway 344. The soldiers opened a gap for him in the razor wire and he passed onto the army side of the line. A lawyer from New York City, he had spent his time inside the Warriors' compound acting as an advisor. Both he and his lawyer believed Mr. Cohen would be asked a few questions and then be allowed to go on his way. They declined the army's offer to take him into military custody. Instead, Mr. Cohen put himself into the hands of the Sûreté du Québec.

He had told the Mohawk that he would be more effective negotiating on their behalf from the outside and that he had received assurances from the army and the police that he would be free to do so. The police promptly arrested him.

SQ officials would not say whether Mr. Cohen would be charged. But his lawyer said he had been led to believe charges of obstruction of justice and participating in a riot would be laid against his client.

Negotiators for the Mohawk holdouts continued to be frustrated in their attempts to talk to the federal or provincial governments. The only line of communication for the people at the TC was the telephone "hotline" which connected them with no one but the military. And the military continued to insist that the only thing left to discuss was when the Warriors would surrender unconditionally. The Mohawk negotiators said they were attempting to find some formula for achieving what they called an "honorable disengagement" to the standoff. All that was required was for the military to grant some sort of face-saving concession, they said. But the Canadian Forces and the governments said they were not interested in hearing those kind of proposals. Surrender, they said, and then we'll talk.

Tuesday, September 25, 1990

The Mohawk made one more offer. The Warriors would lay down their weapons, come out of the treatment center, and surrender themselves into military custody. In return, Québec would agree to appoint a special prosecutor – acceptable to both sides – to decide on what charges could be laid against native people involved in the standoff. There were no more demands for amnesty or the establishment of a joint native/non-native commission to decide on the future of the arrested Warriors. They said they were asking only for the assurance that they would be treated with justice.

Premier Bourassa rejected the offer. He said to accept such a plan would be to discredit Québec's justice system.

Bob Antone, the Oneida who was part of the Mohawk negotiating team, said there would be no more offers from the holdouts. He said they were fed up with being prisoners within their compound, with being cut off from the outside world, and with the endless harassment they faced from the soldiers each night.

The Warriors, he said, would "disengage" by the end of the week no matter what happened.

When darkness fell, the military again began to worry about an escape attempt. During the day, they had strung up barbed wire in the ditches along the TC's perimeter. More spotlights had been hooked up to illuminate the area.

But even with the extra precautions, the soldiers feared that some of the Warriors would try to flee.

Dale — Liberated Women

Dale is a clan mother or Oyaner of the Bear Clan. She was born and raised in Kahnawake. She talks here about women's rights among the Iroquois and The Great Law of Peace:

"The lineal descent of the Iroquois people runs in the female line. Women are considered as progenitors of the nation. They own the land and the soil. Clan mothers solely choose the clan chieftains from the eligible men in the clan. Clan mothers hold all titular rights. There are three for each Mohawk clan, totaling nine. Bear, Wolf and Turtle are the three Mohawk clans. (The other five Iroquois nations have additional clans including Beaver, Deer, Snipe, Heron and Hawk.) It is compulsory to marry outside your own clan. The women help and support the men. In times of strife like these (the 78-day stand-off), they cook and help the men who are on the lines in every way possible.

"The Great Law shows us how to act in the present situation. It is stated that an eagle shall sit on the top of the Tree of Great Peace. (See second law) This eagle is able to see a great distance and if he sees any danger he will at once warn the people who will defend their lands. The eagle is allegorical, meaning the people must be ever watchful. If an outside nation refuses to accept the peaceful way, the Great Law of Peace, they bring war upon themselves. Then the Warriors shall chose a war chief. The current situation is a state of war except that the Warriors are defending their own land. (See thirty-seventh, seventy ninth and eighty first laws.)

"'Warriors' are all the men of the community. They are linked with the Longhouse but warrior is not our word neither is it accurate. Our word is Rotiskarate: it means 'the car-

rier of peace'. They are always prepared to meet their Maker if that's what it takes to defend their people and lands.

"All our effort today is for the younger generations. Their health and happiness is of paramount importance to us. Our Great Law tells us we must think ahead seven generations in making decisions and agreements. We are very much aware of this in these present land negotiations.

"The Longhouse follows the Gayaneshakgowa, the Great Law of Peace or Constitution of the Iroquois, and the Band Council does not. The Band Council has accepted the Indian Act. We have not. The Band Council is elected and funded through the federal government. The Longhouse follows the ancient laws of election of chiefs. Our Constitution is not recognized by the government. The Longhouse recognizes the Two Row Wampum treaty. It was an agreement with the British in 1664. It says that we shall live together in the same land in peace and friendship each under our own law and paddling his own canoe, the other not to interfere or molest his neighbour.

"One aspect of the Iroquois Law that was not copied (in American constitution) were those that established women's rights. Now Americans are trying to pass an Equal Rights Amendment because they ignored the equality of women two-hundred years ago.

"So this attitude still exists in non-Indian peoples and their church and political leaders. The women of the Six Nations feel they were liberated centuries ago with the establishment of the Great Law of Peace."

*Warrior
plays the
"rifle guitar"*

The Warrior known as Blackjack had put together a long stick with a hook at the end. With loud hoots of laughter marking his progress, he made his way along the northern perimeter. Reaching across the razor-wire with his contraption, he yanked on the army tripwires, setting off flares. Each flare sent soldiers scurrying to find out whether a mass breakout was underway.

In a bid to push Blackjack and the other Warriors back from the perimeter, the military resorted to a common crowd-control method. Soldiers hooked up a firehose to a nearby water main. To increase the water pressure, they added a high-powered pump to the line and began spraying the Warriors. But even with the extra pressure, the water was not strong enough to tear down the tarpaulins strung up by the Mohawk to thwart the army spotlights. And the heavy brush prevented the water from penetrating more than a few meters into the forest.

For the Warriors, it was a chance to have some fun. They stashed their weapons behind trees and went up to heckle the soldiers along Highway 344. As the water poured down on them, they called on the soldiers to supply hot water, shampoo and towels. And they spread out along the front where, hidden by the trees, they threw rocks and mimicked the calls of the officers commanding the troops.

Frustrated, the soldiers turned the hose on a television news reporter who was standing out in the open filming the unusual confrontation.

The Mohawk women back at the TC were not about to miss all the fun. They came running up armed with water-filled condoms which the Warriors lobbed through the trees at the soldiers.

Soon, both sides were roaring with laughter. Unamused by the turn of events, an officer gave the order to fix bayonets and to lock-and-load, a term which means to prepare a rifle for firing. The water fight continued.

The officer ordered his men to take cover in a poison ivy-filled ditch facing the front entrance of the TC. One soldier fired a shot into the air. Silence fell upon the area as the Mohawk wondered whether the end was coming. When, after a few minutes nothing had happened, they decided that it was "intermission." They marched back to the TC for coffee and a chance to load up with more water-filled condoms.

Replenished and reloaded, they returned to the front entrance to continue the water fight. But the soldiers had received a dressing down from their officers. They refused to respond to the Warriors. Although the laughter would continue on the Mohawk side for hours afterward, the party was over.

Wednesday, Sept.26, 1990

The tentative plan of the people inside the TC was to lay down their weapons and walk out of the compound at noon the next day. Supporters of the plan argued that the Pines had apparently been saved from the developers, the issue of native rights had been put before the entire world, and there was nothing left to gain by prolonging the holdout. Their principle goals had been met and they could argue that if anyone could be declared the victor in the 78-day-old conflict it was the Mohawk people. There would be no shame in laying down their weapons. It would not be a surrender. They would call it a "unilateral cessation of hostilities."

But some of the Warriors continued to resist the idea.

I'd rather die fighting together with my friends than alone in a police cell, said one Warrior.

Look at what they did to lawyer Stanley Cohen, said another. If they'll double-cross and arrest a white lawyer, what are they going to do to us. What guarantees do we have that we won't be handed straight over to the SQ?

The debate had been going on for days. Some of the Warriors had even begun to doubt the loyalty of the non-Mohawk negotiators such as Bob Antone. They were seeing enemies everywhere.

The Warriors and the other native people at the TC spent the morning arguing back and forth. Two or three times each hour, a Warrior or one of the negotiators would walk up the drive to make a phone call from the "telephone booth." The "booth" was a small area of ground some eight feet by ten feet near the front entrance to the compound. It was the only spot in the entire compound from which, by some quirk of science and nature, cellular phones would function. Everywhere else the phones would be effectively jammed by the military. The Warriors were calling their negotiators on the outside. They were telling them the end was near – perhaps as near as that very evening.

In the early afternoon, the journalists inside the compound were ordered by the Warriors to pack their bags and move up to the front entrance at Highway 344. The Mohawk calls to the outside world became more and more frequent. It was mid-afternoon when the two Warriors known as Hunter and Beekeeper arrived at the front gate and began taking down the tall sapling from which flew the Warrior flag. Once the sapling was down, Hunter cut the leather thongs holding the colors in place. When the last thong had been cut, Hunter and Beekeeper took the flag and began running down the road toward the TC. The journalists sprinted after them. At the TC, they found the Mohawk and their allies preparing to leave. Bags were being packed and men and women had gathered on the front steps. They were celebrating and waving the flags of the Iroquois Confederacy, the Warrior Society, and the Vietnam Veterans association. The children played and laughed and chased each other around the building. In back, two fires were burning. Into the large one, Mohawk threw pieces of disassembled weapons, tapes, papers, and anything else they thought could somehow be used as evidence against them.

Bullets and handguns were dumped into "the Monster" – the Warriors' name for the TC's cesspool

The second fire was the sacred fire. Some of the Mohawk threw tobacco, sweetgrass, and other dried plants into the flames. They chanted prayers in the Mohawk language and sprinkled themselves with ashes scooped from the fire.

The ceremony was presided over by a traditional faith keeper. Suddenly, one of the last of the men who had opposed the idea of the disengagement, Lasagna, appeared. He came forward and the people saw that he was unarmed. They knew then that there would be no one remaining behind to fight it out with the army. The faith keeper opened his arms to Lasagna and the men embraced. Around the fire, men and women alike broke into tears as they too hugged Lasagna.

Burning evidence

Blondie – teenage Warrior

Throughout the ceremony, an army helicopter hovered noisily just off the bluff bordering the southern perimeter of the TC compound. Inside, the soldiers filmed the celebration and the destruction of the weapons.

When the ceremony was over, most of the men, women, and children gathered for a group photo along the edge of the bluff. They laughed and waved their flags as if in victory. The photographers among the journalists snapped away.

Darkness was falling. A Warrior called all the holdouts into the TC for one last meeting. Five minutes later, the Mohawk and their supporters filed out the front door of the treatment center and formed into lines as if for a parade. Women and children took up most of the front ranks. Behind them came the men with the flags. Some of the men carried bodyboards – the hard stretcher-like boards that are used to move people suffering from possible back injuries.

The line set off down the road toward the main gate.

Outside, the soldiers were waiting. Buses with bars welded across the windows were parked at the military camp on the other side of Highway 344. The Mohawk would be quickly processed, put on board the buses and taken to Farnham military base. That was the plan.

But the Mohawk had come up with a plan of their own. They wanted to show the world that they were not surrendering. Their position was that they had done nothing wrong and should not be arrested. It followed, they said, that once they left the TC they should simply head for home.

As their parade reached the half-way point between the TC and the highway, the column suddenly turned right into the forest. Adults picked up the children and carried them through the thick brush. Marching forward, the Mohawk set off some of their own flares. Onward the column went through the smoke and the eerie light thrown out by the sparking flares. When the front of the column reached the razor-wire perimeter, the men threw the body boards on top of the wire. They jumped on the boards, flattening the coils and creating a gap through which they passed onto the broad lawn of the neighboring property.

There were only a few sentries there to meet them. The soldiers shouted for help. Officers barked out orders. The sentries fixed bayonets and soldiers from the army side of the road sprinted across the highway and into the forest in a bid to stop the Mohawk. But there was no way of stopping them. The people in the back of the column could not see what was happening at the front. They continued to push forward.

The ones in the middle were caught as if in the jaws of a human vice. One woman carrying her baby through the gap lost her balance and fell onto the razor wire.

"Help me. Help my baby," she screamed.

Her cries sent the other women into a panic. The men shouted at the soldiers to put away their bayonets and to leave the women and children alone.

A soldier spotted Lasagna and called for help. Together with three other soldiers he wrestled Lasagna to the ground just as the Warrior reached the edge of the highway. As Lasagna and the soldiers scuffled, the rest of the column had also turned left and was marching up toward the road. No one

Soldiers subdue Lasagna

in the Mohawk party ran. As they emerged onto Highway 344, the Mohawk turned right again. They were heading toward the town of Oka.

Taken by surprise, the soldiers fell into disarray. They used their rifle butts to push back the wave of men and women. Children were separated from their parents. They cried out in terror. Mothers screamed for their children. Officers shouted to their men to remain calm and to herd the Mohawk toward the buses. But rather than form up in a line across the road, the soldiers spread out in small, ineffective groups. At least 10 of the holdouts marched straight through the army lines, past the army barricade behind which dozens of journalists were watching, and down the hill toward Oka where most were captured by the waiting Sûreté du Quebc.

It took the soldiers 20 minutes to restore order. The holdouts and the journalists inside the army perimeter were corralled and separated into two groups. The Mohawks' hands were bound with disposable plastic cuffs. They were pushed on board the two buses. They remained defiant, shouting through the windows at the soldiers and unfurling the Warrior flag they had smuggled on board.

The 10 journalists were taken one by one into the army camp to be interrogated by the army and police inside a large military tent surrounded by barbed wire and guarded by dozens of soldiers. Seven were released. Three were carted off to the SQ station in St. Eustache for further questioning. At least one, freelance columnist Albert Nerenberg, was punched and kicked.

Cars bringing people to watch the final moments of the 78-day-old crisis blocked the road into Oka. The military decided to go out the other way. That meant turning the long paddy wagon-school buses around on the two-lane highway. It took another 10 minutes to complete that operation.

At 8:00 p.m., the order was given to move. The buses and their military escort vehicles drove west into the darkness and disappeared around the bend in the highway.

It was the end of the Mohawk revolt at Oka.

Aftermath

The Mohawk standoff began and ended at Kanesatake. But just as they had on the first day, Mohawk of Kahnawake moved on to the Mercier Bridge and the main highways leading into the reserve to protest the treatment of the Warriors at Kanesatake. After witnessing the final scuffle at the TC on their television screens, hundreds of Mohawk at Kahnawake left their homes to confront the soldiers still on their reserve. A crowd of up to 400 Mohawk, some of them armed with baseball bats and rocks, approached six soldiers who were guarding the bridge. The six tried to push the crowd back by firing tear gas. But some of the Mohawk were wearing gas masks. They kept coming forward. Two dozen soldiers arrived to reinforce the position. An officer ordered his men to aim their rifles at the crowd. The action worked. The Mohawk backed off.

While the military was facing down the angry crowd at Kahnawake, Loran Thompson was on his way to the New York state-side of the Akwesasne reserve. One of the more militant members of the traditional Longhouse faction, Thompson had encouraged the holdouts at Kanesatake to hang tough until the end. When the end came, Thompson came out of the

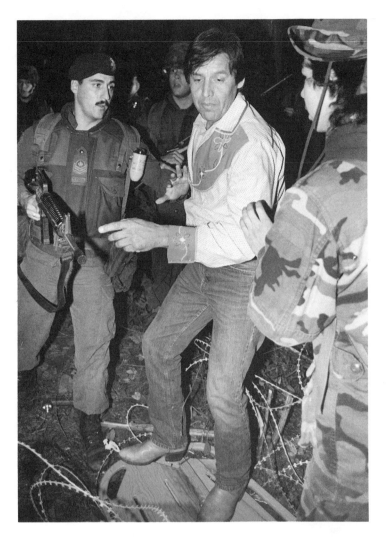

TC with the others. He made it through the army lines and down to the police barrier at the entrance to the town. As he was about to be arrested, the Warrior known as Noriega came marching down the hill dressed in his camouflage gear. In their haste to grab Noriega, the police forgot about Thompson. So he continued on his way. In the town, he found a Mohawk who offered him a lift. By the next day, Thompson was safe on the U.S. side of the frontier at Akwesasne. He spent the weekend with his family. The following Monday, he reported to RCMP headquarters in Westmount as required under the terms of his release on a previous charge of smuggling cigarettes. He was arrested and charged with assaulting a police officer.

Ronald Cross, the Warrior known as Lasagna, appeared in a St. Jerome court the day after the siege ended. He was charged with 22 offenses including assault and uttering death threats. His face was badly bruised and swollen. Police said the marks were the result of a fall Cross had suffered while he was still in the bush by the TC.

In his first comment on the ending of the standoff at Kanesatake, Premier Robert Bourassa said Québecers could be proud that the siege had ended peacefully. But he said that there had been dark episodes in the long affair. And he promised a public inquiry into the government's handling of the crisis.

Mr. Bourassa asked the military to remain on standby at Kahnawake and Kanesatake until security and order had been firmly restored.

Public Security minister Sam Elkas said he still did not know who ordered the failed SQ raid at Kanesatake on July 11th. What's more, he added he didn't want to know. Soon after, he would lose his portfolio in a cabinet shuffle. The job went to Claude Ryan who throughout the crisis had called for the government to use a firm hand in all its dealings with the Mohawk.

The other provincial minister deeply involved in the crisis, John Ciaccia, would also be stripped of his post. As Québec's minister of Native Affairs, Ciaccia had treated the Mohawk with dignity and respect throughout the crisis. At the height of the crisis he allowed the Mohawk of Kahnawake to build a dock on a piece of land he owned in Dorval. The Mohawk used the landing point to load badly-needed food and supplies for the blockaded Kahnawake. But Ciaccia often appeared to be acting without the support of the government. He had no desire to crush the Mohawk. And he had no power to accept any of their demands.

Margaret Gabriel — Politics of Dispair

Married to a Mohawk for thirty years and mother of six (all raised in Oka) and aunt of Ellen, Mrs. Gabriel was born in Folkestone, England and has lived at Kanesatake since 1957. During the isolation of the community by the SQ and later the army, she became a volunteer worker in the emergency committee at the food bank. Her daughter Brenda was in the TC during the entire siege.

"This is a very poor community. Education could be an answer. There is still a high drop-out rate but a lot more are getting a university education now. That's what helps in the negotiations. I don't think the government people expected the young Mohawk to be so bright. And it also surprised them – the role women play.

"Bourassa and his government are stupid. They gave a grant to build the bingo hall and then sent in the SQ to close it down the first day. They smashed everything including the computers. It would have employed 700 people. Most people are against the casino idea because it would bring bad characters into the community, I agree. But bingo? So long as the money comes back into the community, I don't see much morally wrong with bingo. The Québec government raises millions through lotteries. And the Catholic church seems to like the idea. It could have given some employment for the young people and maybe finance some businesses that are needed here.

"This siege has brought the community together. The young

people have seen the governments and police in action against them now. If they are going to arrest everyone that was at the barricade that morning (July 11th) they are going to have to arrest the whole village including me. I think there will

be a movement away from the Band Council to the Longhouse traditions. (Grand Chief) George Martin has no support and most agree he is a puppet for the government and the village of Oka. It was lack of competent

negotiation that led to the impasse on the golf course land."

After the siege was over Margaret Gabriel said: "I feel drained and nothing good seems to be coming out so far. The government is using the internal strife to stall again. Tension is very high. The good thing is I have my daughter back. They fired Linda Simon, the director of the school, and replaced her with someone who just doesn't understand the Mohawk. The Band Council has disbanded the parent committee and there are no budgets for anything. The community wanted a drop-in center to help the healing process but Martin turned it down. They cancelled housing projects and the day care center. They even wanted to send food in the food bank back. They, the Band Council people, were in hotels and well paid. They took $32,000 that was donated to the community for food and medicine and put it in the Band Council's lawyers' trust account. But we need it. There is no employment here and no money earned during the summer. It's going to be a very rough winter for some."

Mohawk activist Kahn-Tineta Horn lost her job at the federal department of Indian Affairs. She also lost custody of her four-year-old daughter. When the siege at Oka began, Horn was on a leave of absence from her job. She was scheduled to return in early September but chose to remain at the TC instead. She was fired for not returning on time. And custody of her daughter, Ganyetahawi, was given to the child's father, lawyer Robert Batt, who accused Horn of endangering his daughter's life by keeping her at the TC. (The court later returned custody to Horn.)

All but a handful of the Mohawk Warriors and supporters involved in the siege at the TC were charged and released on bail. On the night of October 5th, 21 of the men returned to a hero's welcome at Kahnawake. Hundreds of people turned out for the celebration at a local hall. The party lasted long into the night.

In mid-October, federal Indian Affairs minister Tom Siddon announced that a formal settlement of the land dispute at Oka would not come quickly. He blamed it on the Mohawk.

Even before the crisis, there had been deep divisions among the Mohawk of Kanesatake over who spoke for the community. Ottawa recognized the local band council leader George Martin who was elected Grand Chief by nine women known as Clan Mothers. But many of the Mohawk did not support Martin. Some wanted a more democratic system of electing their leader. Others backed the traditionalist Longhouse faction.

When the crisis broke, the anti-Martin forces allied themselves against the Grand Chief. They accused him of deserting the community in its hour of need and of collaborating with the authorities. Martin responded with charges that Warriors from outside Kanesatake had used force and intimidation to coerce the community into opposing him and had needlessly prolonged the standoff.

In Ottawa, Siddon said there would be no negotiations until the two main factions at Kanesatake resolved their differences.

The Mohawk Peacekeeper police force at Kahnawake hired more officers to patrol the reserve and the major highways running through it. But for the first time in more than a decade, the Sûreté du Québec began patrolling the highways as well. Community officials warned that there was little hope for a reduction in tensions as long as members of the Québec police force were on Mohawk land. The Québec government said the police were needed to reassure the people of the surrounding towns that they could use the highways without fear.

On October 13th, some 200 journalists gathered in Montréal to dissect their coverage of the crisis. The consensus was that the Warriors and the military got generally positive coverage because they were usually accommodating to the demands of the press. They gave frequent interviews and hid little from reporters. By contrast, the Sûreté du Québec would only release official statements from its central Montréal office. The result was that the points of view of the military and the Warriors made the headlines often while most of the statements made about the SQ came from the Warriors and their supporters.

It was a situation the SQ officers had difficult accepting during the crisis. The SQ was frequently portrayed as incompetent, brutal, and uncontrollable. The 1,500 officers on duty at Kanesatake and Kahnawake between July 11th and August 20th were verbally and sometimes physically attacked by the non-native population for failing to attack the Mohawk. The Mohawk supporters accused the SQ of wanting to crush the native population.

In frustration, the SQ attempted to blame the local English-language daily, *The Gazette*, for most of its problems. SQ headquarters released a statement accusing *The Gazette* of waging a vendetta against the mainly French-speaking force in retaliation for the failure in June of the Meech Lake constitutional accord which would have granted Québec greater powers. *The Gazette* had, in fact, supported the accord in its editorials, and the bizarre logic of the SQ statement was never adequately explained.

In addition, *The Gazette* had been condemned by the Mohawk as being biased against the native cause. At one point, *Gazette* reporters were temporarily banned by the Mohawk from their territory. So between the SQ and Mohawk attacks, *The Gazette* had a strong case for its claim to having reported impartially on the crisis.

Press interest in the story was also strong outside Québec. Newspapers and TV and radio stations across Canada covered the crisis from beginning to end. And journalists from the United States, Europe, Australia and South America were sent to Oka to report on the standoff.

Both the military and the Mohawk played to the press.

Soldiers on the front lines were on their best behaviour whenever the press was around. The army gave daily press conferences and its press relations officers were always willing to provide interviews and information. Although the military did its best to cut off all communications and supplies for the small group of reporters at the TC during the siege at Oka, the cries of outrage at the violation of press freedom were muted.

The Mohawk did their best to win the hearts and minds of the world by influencing the press coverage. When the blockade of Kahnawake was causing food and fuel shortages in the community, the Mohawk diverted some of their blockade-running boats to bringing reporters to the reserve for press conferences. They cranked out press releases by the dozens and sent them out via fax machines and wire services. In one clever public relations maneouvre, they sent a message to South African anti-apartheid hero Nelson Mandela asking him to call for economic sanctions against Canada in retaliation for its treatment of aboriginal people.

One of the few happy stories to come out of the crisis was the reception given to Mohawk students returning to schools outside Kanesatake and Kahnawake. The general attitude among native and non-native students was that the crisis was the work of adults and there was no reason for any bad feelings among the children.

Women and children, followed by Warriors leave TC, Sept 26, 1990

Soldiers of the Royal 22nd wait on road outside razor

...nter'' tackled to the ground

...s restrain ''Lasagna''

"Splinter" leaves compound with Warrior Flag held high

GAYANESHAKGOWA

GREAT LAW OF PEACE

The Constitution of the Iroquois Confederacy

Introduction

Before the time of Europeans in North America native history records that there was war and strife among the native peoples. Then came the Peacemaker. His message was that people should cease to abuse one another. He pointed out that man alone has the power to reason and should gather together to lay down rules to live by which would ensure peace. He lived among the most warlike Iroquois such as the the People of the Flint (the Mohawk), also the the People of the Standing Stone (the Oneida), the People of the Hills (the Onondaga), the People of the Swamp (the Cayuga), and the People of the Great Hills (the Seneca). These five nations were the first ones to embrace the concepts of the Peacemaker and eventually to gather together in council to find a way towards peaceful coexistance. The result was The Great Law of Peace or the Constitution of the Confederacy of the Iroquois.

It is impossible to overstate the power of thought that came from the study of these Laws. It is unparalleled by any document of political will before or since. Its underlying principle is that since vertical hierachy breeds conflict, the Iroquois must organize their multi-complex society in a way that prevents the internal rise of hierachy.

Then the councillors examined the historical reasons for conflict between them. Noting, for example, that territorial hunting grounds were fought over, they abolished the importance of territories. They welcomed anyone who entered another's territory and guaranteed their safety while there. To replace territorial hunting rights, universal laws of taking and treatment of game were established. All people were free of body, mind and spirit and all had the right to protection under the Great Law of Peace.

These principles of peace were carried further than the absence of conflict. A society had to be developed that was capable of guaranteeing the absence of abuse but yet restrained verticle hierachy. It was of necessity complex. It was therefore required that the people of the Longhouse carried the messages of peace throughout the country. Thus The Great Law not only established a code of conduct devoted to the concept of peace to all men but also laid down the foundations for the government of the modern clan. The Great Law dictated how, when and why to hold meetings, communications between clans and the assignment of titles and appointment of leaders.

When the founding fathers of the United States of America were writing the constitution of their newly-established country, they borrowed liberally from the Great Law. The Senate acknowledged this in 1987 when a select committee on Indian affairs met and later published a written record of their articles of hearing. In it, parallels are drawn between the two documents law by law.

Talking about the parallels between the Iroquois and American nations, Kanesatake faithkeeper Johnny Cree says, "They also took the Iroquois emblem as their national coat of arms with one important difference. The arrows in the talons of the eagle are pointing up on theirs – 'flying.' Ours are turned downward in peace. That is why the Americans have always been at war with other nations and will be till they learn to bury their arms like the Great Law teaches."

These laws were set down around 1539. This English interpretation was compiled from six translations in 1916. The first Grand Councils of the Iroquois included the original five nations: The Mohawk, the Oneida, the Onondaga, the Cayuga, and the Seneca. The Tuscarora, originally from the Carolinas, sought refuge with the Iroquois and were admitted as the Sixth Nation in 1714. The first Grand Councils of the Five Nations were held under the largest white pine in Eastern North America. It stood near Deseronto, Ontario and was more than 250 feet high. It was cut down by white men around 1800.

(This introduction is based in part on the document A Basic Call to Consciousness which the people of the Longhouse presented in September 1977 to the Non-Governmental Organizations of the United Nations in Geneva, Switzerland.)

Editors Note: While several translators have been given credit for the translation from the Indian to English, the "Note" section is, contributed by the renowned poet and historian Louis Karoniaktajeh Hall. The Publishers wish to express their gratitude to Louis Hall for his invaluable expertise and his kindness in allowing the reprinting of his explanatory notes.

1. Deganawida and the Chiefs plant the Tree of Peace

I am Deganawida. With the statesmen of the League of Five Nations, I plant the Tree of the Great Peace. I plant it in your territory, Atotarho and the Onondaga Nation: in the territory of you who are the firekeepers. I name the tree Tsioneratasekowa, the Great White Pine.

Under the shade of this Tree of Great Peace, we spread the soft white feathery down of the Globe Thistle as seats for you, Atotarho and your cousin statesmen. We place you upon those seats, spread soft with the feathery down of the Globe Thistle, there beneath the shade of the spreading branches of the Tree of Great Peace. There shall you sit and watch the Fire of the League of Five Nations. All the affairs of the League shall be transacted at this place before you, Atotarho and your cousin statesmen, by the statesmen of the League of the Five Nations.

2. The Great White Roots of the Tree of Peace

Roots have spread out from the Tree of Great Peace, one to the north, one to the east, one to the south, and one to the west. These are the Great White Roots and their nature is Peace and Strength. If any man or any nation outside of the Five Nations shall obey the laws of the Great Peace (Gayanerekowa) and shall make this known to the statesmen of the League, they may trace back the roots to the Tree. If their minds are clean and if they are obedient and promise to obey the wishes of the League, they shall be welcomed to take shelter beneath the Tree of the Long Leaves.

We place at the top of the Tree of Great Peace an eagle who is able to see afar. If he sees in the distance any danger threatening he will at once warn the people of the League.

Note: The translator got his tree mixed up. Tioneratasekow does not mean a Tree of Long Leaves but a Great Tree with ever fresh leaves meaning evergreen or the Great White Pine. Unless they had domesticated the eagles, it is an allegory, meaning that the people must be very watchful.

3. Atotarho and the Onondaga Chiefs caretakers of the Council Fire

To you and Atotarho and the Onondaga statesmen, I and the other statesmen of the League have entrusted the caretaking and watching of the Five Nations Council Fire. When there is any business to be transacted and the Council is not in session, a messenger shall be sent to either Atotarho, Honowirehton or Skanawati, the firekeepers or their War Chief, with a full statement of the business to be considered. Then Atotarho shall call his cousin chiefs together and consider whether the business is of sufficient importance to call the attention of the Council of the League. If so, Atotarho shall send messengers to summon all the chiefs of the League and to assemble under the Tree of Great Peace. When the statesmen are assembled, the Council Fire shall be kindled but not with chestnut wood and Atotarho shall formally open the Council. Then shall Atotarho and his cousin statesmen, the firekeepers, announce the subject for discussion. The smoke of the Council Fire of the League shall ever ascend and pierce the sky so that the other nations who may be allies may see the council fire of the Great Peace.

Note: Chestnut wood throws out angry sparks. The inference here is not to inspire angry moods. Seeing "The smoke of the Council Fire ascent the sky" is to induce friendly neighbors to "drop in and set a spell."

4. The Firekeepers to keep the Council Fire clean

You, Atotarho and your thirteen cousin statesmen shall faithfully keep the space about the Council Fire clean and you shall allow neither dust nor dirt to accumulate. I lay a long seagull wing (Tiowatstekawe Onerahontsa) before you as a broom. As a weapon against a crawling creature, I lay a stick with you so that you may thrust it away from the Council Fire. If you fail to cast it out, then call the rest of the united statesmen to your aid.

Note: Keeping the space around the council fire clean may also mean that a well conducted council is being recommended and the crawling creature may be a disrespectful person or persons seeking to disrupt the council.

5. The Council of the Mohawks divided into three parties

The Council of Mohawks shall be divided into three parts: Tehanakarineh, Ostawenserenta and Soskohowane are the first. Tekarihoken, Ayonwatha and Satekariwate are the second. Sarenhowane, Teyonhekwen and Orenrekowa are the third. The first party is to listen only to the discussion of the second and third parties and if a error is made or the proceeding

irregular, they are to call attention to it and when the case is right and properly decided by the two parties, they shall confirm the decision of the two parties and refer the case to the Seneca statesmen for their decision. When the Seneca statesmen have decided, in accord with the Mohawk statesmen, the case or question shall be referred to the Cayuga and Oneida statesmen on the opposite side of the house.

Note: The above is the procedure when the Grand Council of the Iroquois Confederacy is in session.

6. Deganawida appoints the Mohawks Chiefs leaders of the Confederacy

I, Deganawida, appoint the Mohawk statesmen the head and the leaders of the Five Nations League. The Mohawk statesmen are the foundation of the Great Peace and it shall therefore be against the Great Binding Law to pass measures in the Council of the League after the Mohawk statesmen have protested against them.

No Council of the League shall be legal unless all the statesmen of the Mohawk are present.

Note: The Mohawks were the first to accept the Great Law. They helped the Founder Deganawida to gather the other nations together. Missionaries admit they went all over America and spread propaganda among the Indians against the Iroquois Confederacy, especially against the Mohawks because they were the "most militant and great organizers." The missionaries felt certain they checked the spread of the Great Law which "would have made it impossible for the white men to conquer America."

7. Onondaga Chiefs open the Council Fire of the Iroquois

Whenever the statesmen of the League shall assemble for the purpose of holding a council, the Onondaga Rotiyaner shall open it by expressing their gratitude to their cousin statesmen and greeting them and they shall make and address and offer thanks to the Earth where men dwell, to the streams of water, the pools and the lakes, to the maize and the fruits, to the medicinal herbs and trees, to the forest trees for their usefulness, and to the animals that serve as food and give their pelts for clothing, to the great winds and to the lesser winds, to the thunderers; to the Sun, the mighty warrior; to the moon; to the messengers of the Creator who reveals his wishes and to the Great Creator who dwells in the heavens above who gives all the things useful to men, and who is the source and the ruler of health and life.

Then shall the Onondaga Rotiyaner declare the Council open.

The Council shall not sit after darkness has set in.

Note: The above opening thanksgiving ritual is done at every gathering of the people. The orator gives thanks to all that help human life. Giving thanks to the trees, water, winds, etc. does not mean that the people worship all these useful gifts but thank the power that produces them.

---

8. Every Onondaga Chief must be present

The Firekeepers shall formally open and close all councils of the statesmen of the League. They shall pass upon all matters deliberated upon by the two sides and render their decision.

Every Onondaga statesman (or his deputy) must be present at every Council of the League and must agree with the majority without unwarrantable dissent, so that a unanimous decision may be rendered.

If Atotarho or any of his cousin statesmen are absent from a Council of the League, any other Firekeeper may open and close the Council, but the Firekeepers present may not give any decisions, unless the matter is of small importance.

Note: No chief may start any unnecessary arguments or unjustifiably delay the progress of the Council.

---

9. All issues first passed by the Mohawks and the Senecas

All the business of the Five Nations League Council shall be conducted by the combined bodies of Confederate statesmen. First the question shall be passed upon by the Mohawk and the Seneca statesmen. Their decision shall be discussed and passed by the Oneida and Cayuga statesmen. Their decision shall then be referred to the Onondaga statesmen, the Firekeepers for final judgment.

The same process shall be followed when a question is brought before the council by an individual or a War Chief.

10. The Cayuga and Oneida chiefs are next to decide

In all cases the procedure must be as follows: when the Mohawk and the Seneca statesmen have unanimously agreed upon a question, they shall report their decision to the Oneida and Cayuga statesmen, who shall deliberate upon the question and report a unanimous decision to the Mohawk statesmen. The Mohawk Rotiyaner will then report the standing of the case to the Firekeepers, who shall render a decision as they see fit in a case of a disagreement by the two bodies or confirm the decisions of the two bodies if they are identical. The Firekeepers shall then report their decision to the Mohawk statesmen who shall announce it to the open Council.

Note: This means that in case of a disagreement between the two parties, Mohawk-Seneca and the Oneida-Cayuga, the Onondaga statesmen shall cast their "vote" on one or the other making it a two thirds majority, making it necessary for the one third minority to go along with the decision of the majority and it becomes a unanimous decision.

---

11. Case must be reconsidered if there is disagreement

If through any misunderstanding or obstinacy on the part of the Firekeepers, they reach a decision at variance with that of the two sides, the Two Sides shall reconsider the matter and if their decisions are jointly the same as before, they shall report to the Firekeepers, who are then compelled to confirm their joint decision.

12. The Oneida Firekeepers are the last to decide

When a case comes before the Onondaga, the Firekeepers, for discussion and decision, Atotarho shall introduce the matter to his comrade statesmen, who shall then discuss it in their two bodies. Every Onondaga statesman except Honowireton shall deliberate and he shall listen only. When a unanimous decision shall have been reached by the two bodies of Firekeepers, Atotarho shall notify Honowireton of the fact, then he shall confirm it. He shall refuse to confirm a decision if it is not unanimously agreed upon by both sides of the Firekeepers.

Note: In the Onondaga national council, the party for the final decision is comprised of only one individual, Honowireton, who however has to follow the rule which is simply to confirm a unanimous decision by saying "I confirm" or "I do not confirm" in case the two sides do not agree. He does not have to take part in the deliberation. It's already taken care of.

13. Chiefs to deliberate in low tones

No chief shall ask a question of the body of chiefs of the League when they are discussing a case, question or proposition. He may only deliberate in a low tone with the separate body of which he is a member.

Note: Such an action by a chief may result in disorder and delay the progress of the council.

14. The Council shall appoint a speaker for the day

When the Council of the Five Nations chiefs shall convene, they shall appoint a speaker for the day. He shall be a chief of either the Mohawk, Onondaga or Seneca nations.

The next day, the Council shall appoint another, but the first speaker may be reappointed if there is no objection, but a speaker's term shall not be regarded more than one day.

15. Only Chiefs have a voice in the Grand Council

No individual or foreign nation interested in a case, question or proposition shall have any voice in the Council of the League except to answer a question put to him by the Speaker of the Chiefs.

Note: This rule precludes hecklers and rowdy disruption.

16. In case a new law is made

If the conditions which shall arise at any future time call for an addition or change to this law, the case shall be carefully considered and if a new beam seems necessary or beneficial, the proposed change shall be decided upon and if adopted, shall be called "Added to the Rafters".

Note: This points out the law-making privileges of the Rotiyaner.

RIGHTS, DUTIES, QUALIFICATIONS OF THE STATESMEN

17. Clan Mothers to hold Chieftainship titles via Wampum Strings

A bunch of certain shell (wampum) strings each two spans in length shall be given to each of the female families in which the chieftainship titles are vested. The right of bestowing the titles shall be hereditary in the family of females legally possessing the bunch of shell strings and the strings shall be the token that the females of the family have the ownership to the chieftainship title for all time to come, subject to certain restrictions mentioned here.

Note: The families mentioned are political families called the "Clan." The women in possession of the Chieftainship title wampum strings are Clan Mothers. Like the Rotiyaner (Chiefs), the Clan Mother can be deposed if she does a serious wrong at which time another woman will be installed in her place as the Clan Mother.

18. Chief deposed if he refuses to attend a Council Fire

If any chief of the league neglects or refuses to attend the Council of the League the other Chiefs of which he is a member shall require their War Chief to request the female sponsors of the Chief so guilty of neglecting his duties to demand his attendance at the Council. If he refuses, the women holding the title shall immediately select another candidate for the title. No chief shall be asked more than once to attend the Council of the League.

Note: The Clan Mother deposes the errant chief. The war Chief recites the words of deposition to the errant chief. Another candidate is selected immediately.

19. An errant Chief deposed by Clan Mother through the War Chief

If at any time it shall be apparent that the chief of the League has not in mind the welfare of the people or disobeys the rules of the Great Law, the men or women of the League, or both jointly, shall come to the Council and scold the erring chief through his War Chief. If the complaint of the people through the War Chief is not heeded on the first occasion, it shall be uttered again and then if no attention is given, a third complaint and warning shall be given. If the chief is still disobedient, the matter shall go to the Council of the War Chiefs. The War Chiefs shall then take away the title of the erring chief by order of the women in whom the title is vested. When the chief is deposed, the women shall notify the chiefs of the League through their War Chiefs and the Chiefs of the League shall sanction the act. The women will then select another of their sons as a candidate and the chiefs shall elect him. Then the chosen one shall be installed by the Installation Ceremony.

When a chief is deposed, his War Chief shall address him as follows: "So you..........., disregard and set at naught the warnings of your women relatives. You fling the warnings over your shoulder to cast them behind. Behold the brightness of the Sun, and in the brightness of the Sun's light, I depose you of your title and remove the emblem of your chieftainship title. I remove from your brow the deer's antlers which was the emblem of your position and token of your nobility. I now depose you and return the antlers to the women whose heritage they are."

The War Chief shall now address the women of the deposed chief and say: "Mothers, as I have deposed your chief, I now return to you the emblem and the title of chieftainship; therefore, repossess them."

Again addressing the deposed chief, he shall say: "As I have deposed and discharged you so you are no longer chief. The rest of the people of the league shall not go with you, for we know not the kind of mind you possess. As the Creator has nothing to do with wrong, so he will not come to rescue you from the precipice of destruction in which you have cast yourself. You shall never be restored to the position you once occupied."

Then shall the War Chief address himself to the Chiefs of the nation to which the deposed chief belongs and say: "Know you, my chiefs, that I have taken the deer's antlers from the brow of.........., the emblem of his position and token of his greatness."

The chiefs of the League shall have no other alternative than to sanction the discharge of the offending chief.

20. For the Chief guilty of murder

If a chief of the League of Five Nations should commit murder, the other chiefs of the nation shall assemble at the place where the corpse lies and prepare to depose the criminal chief. If it is impossible to meet at the scene of the crime the chiefs shall discuss the matter at the next Council of their nation and request their War Chief to depose the chief guilty of the crime, to "bury his women relatives" and to transfer the chieftainship title to a sister family.

The War Chief shall address the chief guilty of murder and say "So you.........., did kill,.........., with your own hands! You have committed a grave crime in the eyes of the Creator. Behold the bright light of the Sun and in the brightness of the Sun's light, I depose you of your title and remove the horns, the sacred emblem of your chieftainship title. I remove from your brow the deer's antlers which was the emblem of your position and token of your nobility. I now depose you and expel you and you shall depart at once from the territory of the League of the Five Nations and never more return again. We, the League of Five Nations, moreover bury your women relatives because the ancient chieftainship title was never intended to have any union with bloodshed, henceforth, it shall not be their heritage. By the evil deed that you have done they have forfeited it forever."

The War Chiefs shall then hand the title to a sister family and shall address it and say: "Our mothers.........., listen attentively while I address you on a solomn and important subject. I hereby transfer to you the ancient chieftainship title for a great calamity has befallen it in the hands of the family of a former chief. We trust you, our Mothers, will always guard it and that you will warn your chief always to be dutiful and to advise his people to live ever in love, peace and harmony that a great calamity may never happen again."

Note: "Bury his women relatives" means political relatives. "Sister Family" is a part of a clan which is composed of three parts, with a Chief and a Clan Mother in each part. The Chieftainship title is lost by the involved part and transferred to another part of the clan. "His women relatives" is that one third part of the clan associated with the deposed killer chief.

21. Certain defects restricts a Chief

Certain physical defects in a statesman of the League makes him ineligible to sit in the League Council. Such defects as infancy, idiocy, blindness, deafness, dumbness, and impotency. When a statesman of the League is restricted by any of these conditions a deputy shall be appointed by his sponsors to act for him, but in cases of extreme necessity, the restricted statesman may exercise his rights.

22. A Chief may or may not resign if active Chiefs refuse to accept his resigntion

If a Statesman of the League desires to resign his title, he shall notify the statesmen of the nation of which he is a member of his intentions. If his co-active statesmen refuse to accept his resignaion, he may not resign his title.

A statesman in proposing to resign may recommend any proper candidate which recommendation shall be received by the statesmen but unless confirmed and nominated by the women who hold the title, the candidate shall not be considered.

23. On Chiefs making Wampum strings or belts

Any chief of the League of Five Nations may construct shell strings or wampum belts of any size or length as pledges or records of matters of national or international importance.

When it is necessary to dispatch a shell string by War Chief or other messenger as a token of summons, the messanger shall recite the contents of the string to whom it is sent. That party shall repeat the message and if there has been a summons he shall make ready for his journey.

Any of the people of the Five Nations may use shells or wampums as a record of a pledge, contract or an agreement entered into and the same shall be binding as soon as shell strings have been exchanged by both parties.

24. The skins of the Chiefs shall be seven spans thick

The chiefs of the League of Five Nations shall be mentors of the poeple for all time. The thickness of their skin shall be seven spans (tsatahniioronkarakeh), which is to say that they shall be proof against anger, offensive action and criticism. Their hearts shall be full of peace and good will, and their minds filled with a yearning for the people of the League. With endless patience, they shall carry out their duty. Their firmness shall be tempered with a tenderness for their people.

Neither their anger nor their fury shall find lodging in their minds and all their words and actions shall be marked by calm deliberation.

25. Chief seeking independent authority will be deposed

If a chief of the League should seek to establish any authority independent of the jurisdiction of the League of the Great Peace, which is the Five Nations, he shall be warned three times in open Council, first by the women relatives, second by the men relatives, and finally by the chiefs of the Nation to which he belongs.

If the offending chief is still persistent, he shall be dismissed by the War Chief of his Nation for refusing to conform to the laws of the Great Peace. His Nation shall then install the candidate nominated by the female name holders of his family.

Note: Again the "relatives" are the people of the Clan, political relatives. The "female name holders of his family" are the Clan Mothers of the Clan. The "name" is the title given to each Royaner while he is going through the ceremony of becoming a Royaner. The title he gets is the name of the original Chief, whose place he assumes when installed as a Royaner.

26. The chiefs as teachers and spiritual guides

It shall be the duty of all the chiefs of the League of Five Nations from time to time as occasion demands to act as teachers and spiritual guides of their people and remind them of their Creator's will and words. They shall say: "Listen, that peace may continue unto future days! Always listen to the words of the Great Creator, for he has spoken. United People, let no evil find lodging in your minds. For the Great Creator has spoken and the Cause of Peace shall not become old. The Cause of Peace shall not die if you remember the Great Creator."

Note: Great faith shown here.

27. All Chiefs must be honest

All the Chiefs of the Five Nations must be honest in all things. They must not be idle and gossip, but be men possessing those honorable qualities that make true leaders. It shall be a serious wrong for anyone to lead a chief into trivial affairs, for the people must ever hold their chiefs high in estimation out of respect to their honorable positions.

A NEW CHIEF

28. A new Chief must make pledge via four strings of wampum

When a candidate Chief is to be installed, he shall furnish four strings of shells or wampum one span in length bound together at one end. Such will constitute the evidence of his pledge to the Chiefs of the League that he will live according to the Constitution of the Great Peace and exercise justice in all affairs.

When the pledge is furnished, the Speaker of the Council must hold the shell strings in his hand and address the opposite side of the Council Fire and he shall begin his address saying: "Now behold him. He has now become a chief of the League. See how splendid he looks."

An address may then follow. At the end of it he shall send the bunch of shell strings to the opposite side and they shall be received as evidence of the pledge. Then shall the opposite side say:

"We now do crown you with the sacred emblem of the deer's antlers, the emblem of your chieftainship. You shall now become a mentor of the people of the Five Nations. The thickness of your skin shall be seven spans, which is to say that you will be with peace and good will. Your mind shall be filled with a yearning for the welfare of the people of the League. With endless patience you shall carry out your duty and your firmness shall be tempered with a tenderness for your people. Neither anger nor fury shall find lodging in your mind. All your words and actions shall be marked with calm deliberation. In all your deliberations in the Council of the League, in your efforts at law-making, in all your official acts, self interest shall be cast away. Do not cast over your shoulder behind you the warnings of your nephews and nieces should they chide you for any error or wrong you may do, but return to the Great Law which is right and just. Look and listen for the welfare of the whole people and have always in view not only the present, but also the coming generations, even those whose faces are yet beneath the surface of the ground – the unborn of the future Nation."

Note: The candidate Chief shall make or buy the required string wampum, four strings of one span (four inches) in length tied together at one end. The Clan Mother keeps the string wampum after the Installation Ceremony. In the addresses, the Royaner holds the string pledge wampum in his hand. The Rotiyaner of the opposite side of the Council Fire from the Candidate Chief shall do the Installation Ceremony. That is, the Mohawk, Seneca and Onondaga Rotiyaner shall be installed by the Oneida and Cayuga Rotiyaner and vice versa.

29. The new chief shall furnish the food for the celebrations

When a chieftainship title is to be conferred, the candidate chief shall furnish the cooked venison, the corn bread and the corn soup, together with other necessary things and the labor for the Conferring of Titles Festival.

30. Chieftainship title can be conferred when the Great Law is recited

The Chiefs of the League may confer the Chieftainship title whenever the Great Law is recited, if there is a candidate, for the Great Law speaks all the rules.

31. A seriously ill Chief is temporarily deposed

If a Chief of the League should become seriously ill and he be thought near death, the women who are the heirs of his title shall go to his house and lift his crown of deer antlers, the emblem of his chieftainship and place them at one side. If the Creator spares him and he rises from his bed of sickness, he may rise with the antlers on his brow.

The following words shall be used to temporarily remove the antlers: "Now our comrade chief, the time has come when we must approach you in your illness. We remove for a time the deer's antlers from your brow. We remove the emblem of your chieftainship title. The Great Law has decreed that no chief should end his life with the antlers on his brow. We therefore lay them aside in the room. If the Creator spares you and you recover from your illness you shall rise from your bed with the antlers on your brow as before and you shall resume your duties as chief of the League and you may again labor for the people of the League."

Note: The Clan Mothers depose a chief before he dies. He must not take the title with him to the grave. The title will be inherited by his successor.

32. No Council for ten days when a Chief dies

If a chief of the League should die while the Council of Five Nations is in session, the Council shall adjourn for ten days. No Council of the League shall sit within ten days of the death of a Chief of the League.

If the Three Brothers (ahsennihontatehkenah) (the Mohawks, the Onondaga and the Seneca) should lose one of their chiefs by death, the Younger Brothers (iatatehkenah) (the Cayuga and the Oneida) shall come to the surviving chiefs of the Three Brothers on the tenth day and console them. If the Younger Brothers lose one of their chiefs, then the Three Brothers shall come to them and console them. And the consolation shall be the reading of the contents of the thirteenth shell wampum of Ayonwatha. At the termination of this rite, a successor shall be appointed by the women heirs of the chieftainship title. If the women are not ready to place their nominee before the chiefs, the Speaker shall say: "Come let us go out." All shall then leave the Council or place of gathering. The Speaker shall lead the way from the house by saying: "Let us depart to the edge of the woods and lie in wait on our bellies." (Tenshakonatioswentarese).

When the women title holders shall have chosen one of their sons, the chiefs of the League will assemble in two places, the Younger Brothers in one place and the three Older Brothers in another. The chiefs who are to console the mourning chiefs shall choose one of their number to sing the Song of Peace as they journey to the sorrowing chiefs, the singer shall lead the way and the chiefs and the people shall follow. When they reach the sorrowing chiefs, they shall hail the candidate chief and perform the rite of Conferring the Chieftainship title. (Ohkeiontentshera)

33. When a Chief dies all Iroquois Chiefs are notified

When a chief of the League dies, the surviving relatives shall immediately dispatch a messenger, a member of another clan, to the Chiefs in another locality. When the runner comes within hailing distance of the locality, he shall utter a sad wail, thusly: "Kwa-ah! Kwa-ah!" The sound shall be repeated three times, and then again and again as many times as the distance may require. When the runner arrives at the settlement, the people shall assemble and one must ask the nature of his sad message. He shall then say: "Let

us consider." (rakwennikon riak). Then he shall tell them of the death of the chief. He shall deliver to them a string of shells or wampum and say: "Here is the testimony, you have heard the message." He then may return home.

It now becomes the duty of the chiefs of the locality to send runners to other localities and each locality shall send messengers until all chiefs are notified. Runners shall travel day and night.

Note: The mourning relatives (members of the same clan) are consoled by the members of the clan that sits opposite to them at the Council Fire. They also do the running to distant chiefs. When their own chief dies then the favor is returned.

34. No Chief may carry his title to the grave

If a chief dies and there is no candidate qualified for the office in the family of the women title holders, the chiefs of the Nation shall give the title into the hands of a sister family (Kentennonteron) in the clan until such time as the original family produces a candidate, when the title shall be restored to the rightful owners.

No chieftainship title may be carried into the grave. The chiefs of the League may dispossess a dead chief of his title even at the grave.

Note: "Sister family in the clan." There are three chiefs and three Clan Mothers in each Clan. Each chief and each Clan Mother represent a "family" or a political family in the Clan. Makes it easy to reach decisions in Clan Councils. The Chieftainship Titles have been in existence since the Confederacy was founded and must not be buried.

35. THE PINE TREE CHIEF

Should any man of the Nation assist with special ability or show great interest in the affairs of the Nation, if he proves himself wise and honest and worthy of confidence, the Chiefs of the League may elect him to a seat among them and he may sit in the Council of the League. He shall be proclaimed a Pine Tree, sprung up for the Nation and be installed as such at the next assembly for the installation of the chiefs. Should he ever do anything contrary to the rules of Great Peace, he may not be deposed from office - no one shall cut him down - but thereafter everyone shall be deaf to his voice and his advice. Should he resign from his seat and title no one shall prevent it. A Pine Tree Chief has no authority to name a successor nor is his title hereditary.

AHSAREKOWA – THE WAR CHIEFS

36. The title names of the Five War Chiefs

The title names of the War Chiefs of the League shall be:

AYONWEHS,
    war chief under Chief Tekarihoken   (Mohawk)
KAHONWAITIRON,
    war chief under Chief Atatsheteh   (Oneida)
AYENTES,
    war chief under Chief Atotarho   (Onondaga)
WENENS,
    war chief under Chief Dekaenyon   (Cayuga)
SHONERATOWANEH,
    war chief under Chief Skanyatariio   (Seneca)

The women heirs of each head chief's title shall be the heirs of the war chief's title of their respective chief.

The war chiefs shall be selected from the eligible sons of the female families holding the chieftainship title.

Note: War Chiefs ruled absolutely over the nations when the Iroquois Confederacy was formed. The ruling War Chiefs were Tekariholen for the Mohawks, Atatsheteh for the Oneidas, Atotarho for the Onondagas, Dekaenyon for the Cayugas and Skanyatariio for the Senecas. They all became part of the 49 Chiefs in the new order devised by Deganawida, Founder of the Iroquois Confederacy. They became Peace Chiefs and a new order for protection and defense was devised and the new category of War Chiefs established and they included Ayonwehs for the Mohawks, Kahonwaitiron for the Oneidas, Ayentes for the Onondagas, Wenens for the Cayugas and Shoneratowaneh for the Senecas and these new War Chiefs took instructions and directions from the former rulers of the nations.

37. One War Chief for each nation – their functions

There shall be one War Chief for each Nation and their duties shall be to carry messages for the chiefs and to take up arms in case of emergency. They shall not participate in the proceedings of the Council, but shall watch its progress and in case of an erroneous action by a chief, the War Chiefs shall receive the complaints of the people and convey the warnings of the women to him. The people who wish to convey messages to the Chiefs of the League shall do so through the War Chief

of their nation. It shall always be his duty to lay the cases, questions and propositions of the people before the Council of the League.

38. When a War Chief dies another is installed

When a War Chief dies, another shall be installed by the same rite as that by which a Chief (of the Council) is installed.

39. When a War Chief acts against the Great Law he is deposed

If a War Chief acts contrary to instructions or against the provisions of the Laws of the Great Peace, doing so in the capacity of his office, he shall be deposed by his women relatives and by his men relatives. Either the women alone or the men alone or jointly may act in such a case. The women title holders shall then choose another candidate.

Note: The people of the Clans here show their power. The women title holders are, of course, the Clan Mothers.

40. When the Chiefs send a messenger for the Council

When the Chiefs of the League take occasion to dispatch a messenger on behalf of the Council of the League, they shall wrap up any matter they may send and instruct the messenger to remember his errand, to turn not aside, but to proceed faithfully to his destination and deliver his message according to every instruction.

41. How the messenger shall proceed

If a message borne by a runner is the warning of an invasion, he shall whoop: "Kwa-ah, Kwa-ah!" twice and repeat at short intervals, then again at a longer interval.

If a human is found dead, the finder shall not touch the body, but return home immediately shouting at short intervals, "Koo-weh!"

KENTARASONHA— THE CLANS

42. Titles of Clans

Among the Five Nations and their decendants there shall be the following Clans: Great Name Bearer, Ancient Name Bearer, Great Bear, Ancient Bear, Turtle, Painted Turtle, Standing Rock, Large Plover, Little Plover (or Snipe), Deer, Pigeon, Hawk, Wolf, Eel, Ball, Opposite side of the Hand and Wild Potatoes. These Clans distributed through their respective nations shall be the sole owners and holders of the soil of the country and in them is vested, as a birthright.

Note: This means that Europeans, not being members of any of these Clans, have no right to own any land in the Iroquois world.

43. Members of the same Clan in other nations are relatives.

People of the Five Nations who are members of a certain clan shall recognize every member of the Clan no matter what Nation, as relatives. Men and women, therefore, who are the members of the same Clan are forbidden to marry.

44. Lineal Descent of the people runs in the female line.

The lineal descent of the people of the Five Nations shall run in the female line. Women shall be considered the Progenitors of the Nation. They shall own the land and the soil. Men and women shall follow the status of their mothers.

45. The Clan Mothers. Women title holders.

The women heirs of the chieftainship titles of the League shall be called Oyaner or Otiyaner for all time to come.

Note: The Clan Mother shall be called Oyaner. Oyaner is derived from the word Oyana meaning "path". Royaner means "He makes a good path for people to follow." Rotiyaner is in the plural. Oyaner is the female "good path maker." Otiyaner is in the plural.

46. Clan Mothers are keepers of the authorized names.

The women of the 48 (now 50) noble families shall be the heirs of the authorized name for all time to come.

When an infant of the Five Nations is given an Authorized Name at the Midwinter Festival or at the Green Corn and the Strawberry and Harvest Festival, one in the cousinhood of which the infant is a member shall be appointed a speaker. He shall announce to the opposite cousinhood the names of the father and mother of the child together with the clan of the mother. Then the speaker shall announce the child's name twice. The uncle of the child shall then take the child in his arms and walking up and down the room shall sing "My head is firm; I am of the League." As he sings the opposite cousinhood shall respond by chanting: "Hyen, Hyen, Hyen, Hyen...." until the song is ended.

Note: The "cousinhood" is the other Clan. The purpose of announcing the Clan of the mother is to point out the Clan of the child. A child is born a Mohawk, Oneida, Onondaga, etc., but when he is named in the Great Law ceremony, the child becomes an Iroquois or Rotinonsonni. He is a Mohawk by blood and an Iroquois by law, for Gayanerekowa, is also known as the Great Law, is the Constitution of the Kanonssonnionwe or the Iroquois Confederacy. By the same token, if an individual or a whole nation leaves the Iroquois Confederacy and in time realize their great error and decides to be reinstated, they would be required to go through the Naming Ceremony or in their case a re-naming ceremony and hold the Pledge Wampum and re-accept the Great Law and this act could be called the Iroquois Pledge of Allegiance.

47. In case the Clan Mothers become extinct

If the female heirs of a title of a chief of the League becomes extinct, the title shall be given by the chiefs of the League to a sister family whom they shall elect, and that family shall hold the name and transmit it to their female heirs, but they shall not appoint any of their sons as a candidate for a title until all the eligible men of the former family shall have died, or otherwise have become ineligible.

Note: If the Clan Mothers who hold a Royaner title become extinct the Chiefs of the Confederacy shall give the Royaner title to another of the three parties making up the Clan but they will not appoint a Royaner until all the eligible men in the former clan (family) have died. Which means that the Chiefs of the Confederacy can institute a new clan if necessary.

48. In case all the Clan Mothers become extinct

If all the heirs to a chieftainship become extinct, and so all the families in the Clan, then the title shall be given by the chiefs of the League to a family of a sister Clan whom they shall elect.

Note: The chiefs shall take from a large clan and make a new clan or keep up the extinct clan so that the title shall not be lost.

49. If a Clan Mother refuses to bestow a chieftainship title

If anyone of the Otiyaner women, heirs of a titleship, shall willfully withhold a chieftainship or other title and shall refuse to bestow it, or if such heirs abandon, forsake or despise their heritage, then shall such women be deemed buried, and their family extinct. The titleship shall then revert to a sister family or Clan, upon application and complaint. The chiefs of the League shall elect the family or Clan which shall in future hold the title.

Note: Political rights are lost by one of the three parties of the Clan when its Clan Mother refuses to follow the rules of her position.

50. Clan Mothers duty if a Chief holds a conference at his home

The Otiyaner women of the League heirs of the chieftainship titles shall elect two women of their family as cooks for the chief when the people shall assemble at his house for business or other purposes.

51. For a Chief holding a conference with other Chiefs at his home

When a chief holds a conference in his home, his wife, if she wishes, may prepare the foods for the union of chiefs who assemble with him. This is an honorable right which she may exercise and an expression of her esteem.

52. How Clan Mothers correct erring chiefs

The Otiyaner women, heirs of the chieftainship titles shall, should it be necessary, correct and admonish the holders of the titles. Those only who attend the Council may do this and those who do not shall not object to what has been said nor strive to undo the action.

Note: The Clan Mothers (Otiyaner) may correct and give friendly advice to the Rotiyaner (Chiefs).

53. Rules for Clan Mothers to follow in selecting a new Chief

When the Otiyaner women, holders of the chieftainship title, select one of their sons as a candidate, they shall select one who is trustworthy, of good character, of honest disposition, one who manages his own affairs, and supports his own family, if any, and who has proven a faithful man to his family.

Note: When the Clan Mothers "select one of their sons" it means one of the men in the Clan who has the proper qualifications. It does not necessarily mean one of their own natural sons, the Clan being a political family.

54. Clan Mothers hold a council to select a new chief

When a chieftainship title becomes vacant through death or other cause, the Otiyaner women of the Clan in which the title is hereditary shall hold a council and shall choose one of their sons to fill the office made vacant. Such a candidate shall not be the father of any chief of the League. If the choice is unanimous, the name is referred to the relatives of the Clan. If they should disapprove it shall be their duty to select a candidate from among their own number. If then the men and women are unable to decide which of the two candidates shall be named then the matter shall be referred to the chiefs of the League in the Clan. They shall decide which candidate shall be named. If the men and women agree to the candidate, then his name shall be referred to the sister clan for confirmation. If the sister clans confirm the choice, they shall refer their action to the chiefs of the League who shall ratify the choice and present it to their cousin chiefs, and if the cousin chiefs confirm the name, then the candidate shall be installed by the proper ceremony for the conferring of chieftainship titles.

Note: Again "one of their sons" means the eligible men of the Clan. The new chief shall have to meet with the approval of all the men, women, Clan Mothers and other Chiefs.

THE SYMBOLS

55. All Chiefs contribute to the making of the Grand Council Wampum Strings

A large bunch of shell strings, in the making of which the Five Nations League Chiefs have equally contributed, shall symbolize the completeness of the union, and certify the pledge of the Nations, represented by the chiefs of the League of the Mohawk, the Oneida, the Onondaga, the Cayuga and the Seneca, that all are united and formed into one body, or union, called the Union of the Great Law which they have established.

A bunch of shell strings is to be the symbol of the Council Fire of the League of Five Nations. And the chief whom the Council of Firekeepers shall appoint to speak for them in opening the Council shall hold the strands of shell in his hands when speaking. When he finishes speaking, he shall place the strands on an elevated place or pole so that all the assembled chiefs and the people may see it and know that the Council is open and in progress.

56. Each Wampum String represents one territory of the Nations

Five strings of shell tied together as one shall represent the Five Nations. Each string shall represent one territory and the whole a completely united territory known as the Five Nations Territory.

57. Five arrows bound together "united in one body and one mind"

Five arrows shall be bound together very strong and shall represent one Nation each. As the five arrows are strong bound, this shall symbolize the complete union of the nations. Thus are the Five Nations completely united and enfolded together, united into one head, one body and one mind. They therefore shall labor, legislate and council together for the interest of future generations.

Note: When the Confederacy was formed, Deganawida actually demonstrated by taking one arrow and breaking it in half. Then he took five arrows and tried to break it to show how strong the Five Nations can become.

58. Any Chief or other persons who submit to laws of a foreign people are alienated and forfeit all claims in the Iroquois nations

There are now the Five Nations League Chiefs standing with joined hands in a circle. This signifies and provides that should any of the chiefs of the League leave the Council and the League, his crown of antlers,

the emblem of his chieftainship title, together with his birthright, shall lodge on the arms of the union chiefs whose hands are so joined. He forfeits his title and the crown falls from his brow, but it shall remain in the League.

A further meaning of this is that if, at any time, anyone of the chiefs of the League choose to submit to the law of a foreign people, he is no longer in but out of the League and the persons of this class shall be called "They have alienated themselves" (Tehonatonkonton). Likewise, such persons who submit to laws of foreign nations shall forfeit all birthrights and claims of the League of Five Nations and territory.

You, the League of Five Nations Chiefs, be firm so that if a tree should fall upon your joined hands, it shall not separate you or weaken your hold. So, shall the strength of union be preserved.

Note: This means that the Indians who follow the laws made by foreigners, including, Canada's Indian Act and the U.S. Federal Indian Law have alienated themselves from their own nations. That is why Indians such as Mohawk who voted in the elections devised by the Canadian or U.S. governments, have to be reinstated in a special ceremony to regain their lost Iroquois citizenship which they lost by the simple act of voting in the Canadian Council or U.S. Tribal Council elections as well as voting in Canada's national or the U.S. national elections.

59. In case any or all chiefs go against the Great Law, they may either be deposed or executed by the War Chief and his men

A bunch of Wampum strings, three spans of the hand in length, the upper half of the bunch being white and the lower half black and formed from equal contributions of the men of the Five Nations, shall be the token that the men have combined themselves into one head, one body and one thought, and it shall symbolize their ratification of the peace pact of the League, whereby the Chiefs of the Five Nations have established the Great Peace. The white portion of the shell strings represents the women and the black portion the men. The black portion, furthermore, is a token of power and authority vested in the men of the Five Nations.

This string of wampum vests the people with the right to correct their erring chiefs. In case a part of the chiefs or all of them pursue a course not vouched for by the people and heed not the third warning of their women relatives (Waswnensawenrate), then the matter shall be taken to the general council of the Women of the Five Nations. If the chiefs notified and warned three times fail to heed, then the case falls into the hands of the men of the Five Nations. The War Chiefs shall then by right of such power and authority, enter the open Council to warn the chief or chiefs to return from their wrong course. If the chiefs heed the warning, they shall say: "We shall reply tomorrow." If then an answer is returned in favor of justice and in accord with Great Law, then the Chiefs shall individually pledge themselves again, by again furnishing the necessary shells for the pledge. Then shall the War Chief of Chiefs exhort the chiefs, urging them to be just and true.

Should it happen that the chiefs refuse to heed the third warning then two courses are open: either the men may decide in their council to depose the chief or chiefs, or to club them to death with war clubs. Should they in their council decide to take the first course, the War Chief shall address the chief or chiefs saying:

"Since you the chiefs of the Five Nations have refused to return to the procedure of the Constitution, we now declare your seats vacant and we take off your horns, the token of your chieftainship, and others shall be chosen and installed in your seats. Therefore, vacate your seats."

Should the men in their council adopt the second course, the War Chief shall order his men to enter the Council, to take positions beside the errant chiefs sitting between them wherever possible. When this is accomplished the War Chief holding in his outstretched hand a bunch of black wampum strings shall say to the erring chiefs.

"So now, Chiefs of the Five Nations harken to these last words from your men. You have not heeded the warnings of the General Council of Women and you have not heeded the warnings of the Men of the Nations, all urging you to the right course of action. Since you are determined to resist and to withhold justice from your people, there is only one course for us to adopt."

At this point, the War Chief shall drop the bunch of black wampum and the men shall spring to their feet and club the erring chiefs to death. Any erring chief may become submissive before the War Chief lets fall the Black Wampum.

The Black Wampum here used symbolizes that the power to execute is buried, but it may be raised up again by the men. It is buried, but when the occasion arises, they may pull it up and derive their power and authority to act as here described.

Note: The right to decide on execution is held by both the General Council of the Men of the Five Nations and the General Council of the Women of the Five Nations. So is the right to decide on war. The "War Chief shall order his men." In the present century a new title has been given to the War Chief and his men: "The Warrior Society."

60. Wampum Belt of the Iroquois Confederacy

A broad belt of wampum of thirty-eight rows, having a white heart in the center, on either side of which are two white squares all connected with the heart by white rows of beads shall be the emblem of unity of the Five Nations.

The first of the squares on the left represents the Mohawk Nation and its territory, the second square on the left and near the heart represent the Oneida Nation and its territory, and the white heart in the middle represents the Onondaga Nation and its territory. It also means that the heart of the Five Nations is single in its loyalty to the Great Peace, and that the Great Peace is lodged in the heart (meaning with Onondaga League Chiefs) and that the Council Fire is to burn there for the Five Nations. Further it means that the authority is given to advance the cause of peace whereby hostile nations out of the League shall cease warfare. The white square to the right of the heart represents the Cayuga Nation and its territory and the fourth and last square represents the Seneca Nation and its territory.

White here symbolizes that no evil nor jealous thoughts shall creep into the mind of the chiefs while in Council under the Great Peace. White, the emblem of peace, love, charity and equity surrounds and guards the Five Nations.

Note: The above Wampum Belt was made by Ayonwatha (Hiawatha to the white man) to commemorate the making of the Great Law.

6l. In case a great Calamity threatens

Should a great calamity threaten the generations rising and living of the Five Nations, then he who is able to climb to the top of the Tree of the Great Long Leaves (White Pine) may do so. When he reaches the top of the Tree, he shall look about in all directions and should he see evil things indeed approaching, then he shall call to the people of the Five United Nations assembled beneath the Tree of the Great Peace and say: "A calamity threatens your happiness."

Then shall the Chiefs convene in Council and discuss the impending evil, when all the truths relating to the trouble shall be fully known and found to be truths, then shall the people seek a tree of Kahonkaahkona, the great swamp elm tree and when they shall find it they shall assemble their heads together and lodge for a time between its roots. Then, their labors being finished, they may hope for happiness for many days after.

62. Reading the Great Law

When the League of the Five Nations Council declares for a reading of the belts of shell to mind these laws, they shall provide for the reader a specially made mat woven of the fibers of wild hemp. The mat shall not be used again, for such formality is called "honoring the importance of the law."

Note: The reading of the Great Law from the Wampum is very important and honorable. Some Indians won't read the Great Law in its written form because it says it should be recited every five years from the Wampum records. That's the way it had to be done originally because there was no written language. Now that there is a written language, Deganawida would have certainly recommended and urged that the people read the Great Law often. There are chiefs who don't even know when they are violating the law because they refuse to read it in its written form.

63. How the Great Law is recited

Should two sons of opposite sides of the Council Fire agree (iatawa) in a desire to hear the reciting of the laws of the Great Peace and so refresh their memories in a way specified by the Founder of the League, they shall notify Atotarho. He shall consult with five of his cousin chiefs and they in turn shall consult with their eight brethren. Then should they decide to accede to the request of the two sons from the opposite sides of the Council Fire, Atotarho shall send messengers to notify the Chief of each of the Five Nations. Then they shall dispatch their War Chief to notify their brother and cousin chiefs of the meeting and its time and place.

When all have come and have assembled, Atotarho in conjunction with his cousin chiefs, shall appoint one chief who shall repeat the laws of the Great Peace to the two sons. Then the chosen one shall repeat the laws of the Great Peace.

Note: "Two sons of opposite sides of the Council Fire" means two ordinary men, non-chiefs who are members of different clans who

sit opposite each other across the Council Fire. Atotarho's "five cousin chiefs" means those who sit opposite him in the Onondaga Council. "Their eight brethren" means brother Chiefs who sit on the same side of the Council Fire. It would seem that the Wampum reader repeats, that is reads the Great Law twice, once to the two sons and then to everybody.

64. The expert Speaker/Singer of the Law at the Installation Rites

At the ceremony of the installations of chiefs, if there is only one expert speaker and singer of the Law and the Song of Peace to stand at the Council Fire, then when this speaker and singer has finished addressing one side of the Fire, he shall go to the opposite side and reply to his own speech and song. He shall act for both sides of the Fire until the entire ceremony has been completed. Such a speaker and singer shall be termed "Two-faced" because he speaks and sings for both sides of the Fire

Note: People can become lax and negligent and suddenly find themselves without the right kind of speakers and singers.

65. Burying the weapons ceremony

I, Deganawida, and the United Chiefs, now uproot the tallest tree (Skarenhesekowa) and into the hole thereby made we cast all weapons of war. Into the depths of the earth, down into the deep underneath currents of water (Tionawatetsien) flowing to unknown regions we cast all the weapons of strife. We bury them from sight and we plant again the tree. Thus shall the Great Peace be established and hostilities shall no longer be known between the Five Nations but peace to the United People.

Note: The Five Nations buried their weapons of war so they would never fight and kill each other again and they haven't. They only unbury the war club to execute a traitor. However, they did not bury the hatchet to all their enemies for they fought numerous wars and battles after the Iroquois Confederacy was founded and the Great Law was established.

ADOPTIONS

66. "A name hung about the neck"

The father of a child of great comeliness, learning ability or specially loved because of some circumstances may, at the will of the child's Clan, select a name from his own (the father's) Clan and bestow it by ceremony, such as is provided. The naming is only temporary and shall be called "A name hung about the neck."

Note: A given name can be only temporary.

67. Giving a name to a person of another Clan or a foreign nation

Should any person, a member of the League of Five Nations, especially esteem a man or a woman of another Clan or of a foreign nation, he may choose a name, bestow it upon that person so esteemed. The naming shall be in accord with the ceremony of bestowing names. Such a name is only temporary and shall be called "A name hung about the neck". A short string of shells shall be delivered with the name as a record and a pledge.

Note: This type of name giving is more serious as a string wampum and a pledge are involved.

68. Asking to be adopted into a Clan

Should any member of the Five Nations, a family or a person belonging to a foreign nation submit a proposal for adoption into a Clan or one of the Five Nations, he or she shall furnish a string of shells, a span in length, as a pledge to the Clan into which he or they wish to be adopted. The Chiefs of the Nation shall then consider the proposal and submit a decision.

Note: Adoption is how the Clans are kept at full strength.

69. For one to adopt a person, a family or a number of families

Any member of the Five Nations, who through esteem or other feelings, wishes to adopt an individual, a family or a number of families, may offer adoption to him or them and if accepted, the matter shall be brought to the attention of the Chiefs for confirmation and the Chiefs must confirm the adoption.

Note: Anyone may adopt a person or many persons but must get official sanction by the Rotiyaner in Council.

70. What to do after adoption

When the adoption of anyone shall have been confirmed by the Chiefs of the Nation the chiefs shall address the people of the Nation and say:

"Now you of our Nation be informed that..................(such a person, such a family or such families) have ceased forever to bear their birth nation's name and have buried it in the depth of the earth. Henceforth let no one of our nation ever mention the original name or nation of their birth. To do so will hasten the end of our peace." The name of the adopted person's nation or birth place must never be mentioned as it causes trouble or end of the peace.

EMIGRATION

71. About emigrating to a distant region

When a person or family belonging to the Five Nations desires to abandon their Nation and the territory of the Five Nations they shall inform the Chiefs of their nation and the Council of the League of Five Nations shall take notice of it.

When any person or any of the people of the Five Nations emigrate and reside in a distant region away from the territory of the League of Five nations, the chiefs of the Five Nations at will may send a messenger carrying a broad belt of black shells and when the messenger arrives he shall call the people together or address them personally displaying the belt of black shells and they shall know that this is an order for them to return to their original homes and to their Council Fires.

Note: The Rotiyaner may or may not recall an emigrant depending on the circumstances.

FOREIGN NATIONS

72. Law of ownership

The soil of the earth from one end to the other is the property of people who inhabit it. By birthright, the Onkwehonwe, the original beings, are the owners of the soil which they own and occupy and none other may hold it. The same law has been held from the oldest times.

Note: The Onkwehonwe legal opinion is that the natives of America were the first humans on this land. They originated in the land they live on and occupy and no foreigners have the right to take over the land. The so-called "conquest of America" is simply a bare-faced robbery of Indian land.

73. People made different, put in different lands and speak different languages

The Great Creator has made us of one blood and of the same soil he made us, and as only different tongues constitute different nations, he established different hunting grounds and territories and made boundary lines between them.

Note: Each nation has a boundary line to stay within. Also no race of people has a "God given" right to invade other races.

74. Alien nations admitted on a temporary basis

When any alien or individual is admitted into the League the admission shall be understood only to be a temporary one. Should the person or nation create loss or do wrong, cause suffering of any kind to endanger the peace of the League, the League statesmen shall order one of their War Chiefs to reprimand him or them. If a similar offense is committed, the offending party shall be expelled from the League.

75. Alien refugee seeking permanent residence

When a member of an alien nation comes to the territory of the League and seeks refuge amd permanent residence, the Statesmen of the Nation to which he comes shall extend hospitality and make him a member of the Nation. Then he shall be accorded equal rights and privileges in all matters except as mentioned here.

76. Temporary adoptions

No body of alien people who have been adopted temporarily shall have a vote in the Council of the Chiefs of the League, for only they who have been invested with chieftainship titles may vote in the Council. Aliens have nothing by blood to make claim to a vote and should they have it, not knowing all the

traditions of the League, might go against the Great Peace. In this manner, the Great Peace would be endangered and perhaps be destroyed.

Note: The word "vote" is used here to mean "voice" as there is no voting or balloting in the National or Grand Councils of the Five Nations. Only the Rotiyaner have a voice in the Councils unless an individual is asked to speak by the Rotiyaner.

77. The temporary adopted may also be expelled

When the chiefs of the League decide to admit a foreign nation and an adoption is made, the chiefs shall inform the adopted nation that its admissiom is only temporary. They shall also say to the nation that it must never try to control; to interfere with or to injure the Five Nations, nor disregard the Great Peace or any of its rules or customs. In no way should they cause disturbance or injury. Then shall the adopted nation disregard these injunctions, their adoption will be annulled and they will be expelled.

The expulsion shall be in the following manner; the Council shall appoint one of their War Chiefs to convey the message of annulment amd he shall say: "You, (naming the nation), listen to me while I speak. I am here to inform you again of the will of the Five Nations Council. It was clearly made known to you at a former time. Now the chiefs of the Five Nations have decided to expel you and cast you out. We disown you now and annul your adoption. Therefore you must look for a path in which to go and lead away all your people. It was you, not we, who committed wrong and caused this sentence of annulment. So then go your way and depart from the territory of the Five Nations and away from the League."

Note: The Tuscaroras were admitted into the Iroquois Confederacy in 1714 and given a piece of Oneida territory. It was too close to white settlements and they asked for land farther away and so were given land in Seneca territory. They are not a foreign Indian nation. They had found their way back to their own people. A different situation would exist if an alien Indian nation living in their own territory asked to join the Iroquois Confederacy which was the original plan of Deganawida, to have all Indian nations unite in one big alliance. They never got beyond Five Nations. The Tuscaroras were not given a voice in the Grand Council and all other Indian nations seeking admission were given protectorate Indian nation status with no voice nor power in the Confederacy, not what Deganawida had in mind at all. Had his plan been followed there would now be a mighty Iroquois Confederacy of more than 200 nations with a country of its own. The missionaries take the credit for this failure to create a pan-american Confederacy. They say they went all over America to all Indian nations and spread propaganda against the Iroquois Confederacy, especially against the Mohawks who they consider the most militant and most able organizers.

78. Foreign nations urged to accept the Great Peace

Whenever a foreign nation enters the League or accepts the Great Peace, the Five Nations and the foreign nation shall enter into an agreement and compact by which the foreign nation shall endeavor to persuade the other nations to accept the Great Peace.

Note: They asked other nations to help spread peace among mankind.

WAR

79. About War and having the men (Warrior Society) ready

Skanawadi shall be vested with a double office, duty and double authority. One half of his being shall hold the statesman title and the other half shall hold the title of War Chief. In the event of war he shall notify the five War Chiefs of the League and command them to prepare for war and have the men ready at the appointed time and place for engagement with the enemy of the Great Peace.

Note: At the time the Confederacy was formed, all chiefs were war chiefs and this included Skanawadi, Tekarihoken, etc. After the new order of things, the War Chiefs became a part of the National and Grand Council until they died and afterwards, the War Chiefs became a separate entity.

80. Establishing the Great Peace on an outside nation by force

When the Council of the League has for its object the establishment of the Great Peace among the people of an outside nation and that nation refuses to accept the Great Peace, then by such refusal they bring a declaration of war upon themselves from the Five Nations. Then shall the Five Nations seek to establish the Great Peace by a conquest of the rebellious nation.

81. The men of the League (Warrior Society) choose which of the War Chiefs to lead them in battle

When the men of the League, now called forth to become warriors, are ready for battle with an obstinate opposing nation that has refused to accept the Great Peace, then one of the five War Chiefs shall be chosen by the warriors of the League to lead the army into battle. It shall be the duty of the War Chief so chosen to come before his warriors and address them. His aim shall be to impress upon them the necessity of good behavior and strict obedience to the commands of the War Chiefs.

He shall deliver an oration exhorting them with great zeal to be brave and courageous and never to be guilty of cowardice. At the conclusion of his oration he shall march forward and commence a War Song and he shall sing:

Onen onkehnenrenneh	Now I am greatly surprised
Ne kahti enkatieratakwe	And therefore I shall use it
Tsiniwakerennotenne	The power of my war song
Wisk Niwakonwentsakeh	I am of the Five Nations
Ento kahti yenkeriwaneken	And I shall make an appeal
Rahonha ne Rohsatstenserowanen	To the Mighty Creator
Ne rakwawi ne kahti ne akitiokwa	He has furnished this army
Rotiskenrakete ne kati ese	My warriors shall be mighty
Sashatstenserowanen	In the strengh of the Creator
Tookenshen nih sonneh	Between him and my song they are
Ne kati ne takwawi	For it was he who gave the song
Ne karenna enkaterennoten	This war song that I sing

Note: The warriors choose the War Chief and they also choose which of the War Chiefs shall lead them in the war.

82. How the War Party approaches the enemy

When the warriors of the Five Nations are on an expedition against the enemy, the War Chief shall sing the War Song as he approaches the country of the enemy and not cease until his scouts have reported that the army is near the enemy lines when the War Chief shall approach with great caution and prepare for the attack.

83. After the War

When peace shall have been established by the termination of the war against a foreign nation, then the War Chief shall cause all the weapons of war to be taken from the nation. Then shall the Great Peace be established and that nation shall observe all the rules of the Great Peace for all time to come.

84. The conquered nation may continue their form of government

Whenever a foreign nation has been conquered or has by their own will accepted the Great Peace, their own system of internal government may continue, but they must cease all warfare against other nations.

85. When an obstinate enemy is exterminated

Whenever a war against a foreign nation is pushed until the nation is about to be exterminated because of its refusal to accept the Great Peace and if that nation shall by its obstinacy become exterminated, all their rights property and territory shall become the property of the Five Nations.

86. A symbolic relationship established

Whenever a foreign nation is conquered and the survivors are brought into the territory of the League of Five Nations and placed under the Great Peace, the two shall be known as the Conqueror and the Conquered. A symbolic relationship shall be devised and be placed in some symbolic position. The conquered nation shall have no voice in the councils of the League in the body of chiefs.

87. Terms of Peace

When the war of the Five Nations on a foreign rebellious nation is ended, peace shall be restored to that nation by a withdrawal of all their weapons of war by the War Chief of the Five Nations. When all the terms of peace shall have been agreed upon, a state of friendship shall be established.

88. The Great Peace urged on foreign nation by persuasion or by force

When the proposition to establish the Great Peace is made to a foreign nation it shall be done in mutual council. The foreign nation is to be persuaded by reason and urged to come into the Great Peace. If the Five Nations fail to get the consent of the nation at the first council, a second council shall be held and upon a

second failure, a third council shall be held and this third council shall end the peaceful methods of persuasion. At the third council, the War Chief of Five Nations shall address the chief of the foreign nation and request him three times to accept the Great Peace. If refusal steadfastly follows, the War Chief shall let the bunch of white lake shells drop from his outstretched hand to the ground and shall bound quickly forward and club the offending chief to death. War shall thereby be declared and the War Chief shall have his warriors to back any emergency. War must continue until the contest is won by the Five Nations.

89. A peace Chief on diplomatic mission accompanied by Warriors

When the chiefs of the Five Nations propose to meet in conference with a foreign nation with proposals for an acceptance of the Great Peace, a large band of Warriors shall conceal themselves in a secure place safe from the espionage of the foreign nation but as near at hand as possible. Two warriors shall accompany the Union Chief who carries the proposals and these warriors shall be especially cunning. Should the chief be attacked, these warriors shall hasten back to the army of warriors with the news of the calamity which fell through the treachery of the foreign nation.

90. A Peace Chief must renounce his title to go to war

When the Five Nations Council declares war, any chief of the League may enlist with the warriors by temporarily renouncing his sacred chieftainship title which he holds through the nomination of his women relatives. The title then reverts to them and they may bestow it upon another temporarily until the war is over, when the chief, if living, may resume his title and seat in the council.

Note: The Royaner turned warrior cannot exert any authority in the field of action and must take orders from the War Chief like any other warrior.

91. A Wampum Belt of black beads is the emblem of the five War Chiefs

A certain wampum belt of black beads shall be the emblem of the authority of the five War Chiefs to take up the weapons of war and with their men to resist invasion. This shall be called a war in the defense of the Territory.

92. If a part of a nation, a whole nation or more than a nation endeavor to destroy the Great Peace by violating the laws, they shall be driven from the territory by the War Chief and his men (Warrior Society)

If a nation, part of a nation, or more than one nation within the Five Nations should in any way endeavor to destroy the Great Peace by neglect or violating its laws and resolve to dissolve the League, such a nation or nations shall be deemed guilty of treason and called enemies of the League and the Great Peace.

It shall then be the duty of the chiefs of the League who remain faithful to resolve to warn the offending people. They shall be warned once and if a second warning is necessary, they shall be driven from the territory of the League by the War Chief and his men.

RIGHTS OF THE PEOPLE

93. The referendum. The people decide on the most important matters

Whenever an especially important matter or a great emergency is presented before League Council and the nature of the matter effects the entire body of Five Nations threatening their utter ruin, then the chiefs of the League must submit the matter to the decision of their people and the decision of the people shall effect the decision of the League Council. This decision shall be a confirmation of the voice of the people.

94. The men of every Clan shall hold a council and their decision shall be considered by the Council of Chiefs

The men of every Clan of the Five Nations shall have a Council Fire ever burning in readiness for a Council of the Clan. When it seems necessary for the interest of the people, for a council to be held to discuss the welfare of the Clan, then the men may gather about the fire. This council shall have the same rights as the Council of Women.

95. The Council Fires of the women of every Clan have the same rights as the councils of the men

The women of every Clan of the Five Nations shall have a Council Fire ever burning in readiness for a council of the Clan. When in their opinion it seems necessary for the interest of the people, they shall hold a council and their decision and recommendation shall be introduced before the Council of Chiefs by the War Chief for its consideration.

96. All the Clan Council Fires of a Nation or the Five Nations may unite into one General Council Fire

All the Clan Council Fires of a Nation or of the Five Nations may unite into one general Council Fire, or delegates from all the Council Fires may be appointed to unite in a general Council for discussing the interest of the people. The people shall have the right to make appointments and to delegate their power to others of their number. When their council shall have come to a conclusion on any matter their decision shall be reported to the Council of the Nation or the League Council (as the case may require) by the War Chief or the War Chiefs.

Note: The League Council is also known as the Grand Council. When the people of the Iroquois Confederacy hold a general council, the Grand Council has to go along with their decision as the Confederacy is a people's government.

97. Original National Council Fires shall continue

Before the real people united their nations, each nation had its own Council Fires. Before the Great Peace their councils were held. The Five Council Fires shall continue to burn as before and they are not quenched. The chiefs of each Nation in the future shall settle their national affairs at this Council governed always by the laws and rules of the Council of the League and the Great Peace.

98. Rights of the ordinary man and woman

If either a nephew or a niece see an irregularity in the performance of the functions of the Great Peace and its laws, in the League Council or in the Conferring of

Chief titles in an improper way, through their war Chief they may demand that such actions become subject to correction, and that the matter conform to the ways prescribed by the law of the Great Peace.

Note: The "nephew" and "niece" means ordinary men and women who are not Rotiyaner or Clan Mothers, showing that every one has the right to correct any wrong being done. The Great Peace and the Great Law seem to be interchangeable. Each is a product of the other.

99. The ceremonies to continue

The rites and festivals of each nation shall remain undisturbed and continue as before, because they were given by the people of old times as useful and necessary for the good of men.

100. The Midwinter Thanksgiving Festival

It shall be the duty of the chiefs of each brotherhood to confer at the approach of the time of the Midwinter Thanksgiving and to notify the people of the approaching festival. They shall hold a council over the matter, arrange its details and begin the Thanksgiving five days after the moon of Tiskonah is new. The people shall assemble at the appointed place and the nephews shall notify the people of the time and place. From the beginning to the end the chiefs shall preside over the Thanksgiving and address the people from time to time.

Note: The Midwinter Festival begins five days after the new moon following the Winter Solstice. The "nephews" are runners who go to inform the people of the time of the Festival.

101. List of Thanksgiving festivals

It shall be the duty of the appointed managers of the Thanksgiving festivals to do all that is needful for carrying out the duties of the occasions.

The recognized festivals of Thanksgiving shall be the Midwinter Thanksgiving, the Maple or Sugarmaking Thanksgiving, the Raspberry Thanksgiving, the Strawberry Thanksgiving, the Cornplanting Thanksgiving, the Cornhoeing Thanksgiving, the Little Festival of Green Corn, the Great Festival of Ripe Corn and the complete Thanksgiving for the Harvest. Each nation's festivals shall be held in their Longhouses.

Note: The translator from the Indian to English must have consulted the wrong authority. After the Maple Festival (first food by nature of the year), the Planting Festival is next. The medicinal herbs show themselves, the first fruits the Strawberry appears. The next is the first of the field products, the Bean Festival, then the Green Corn and then the Harvest Festival. This writer (Louis Hall) in 25 years of attending the festivals, never saw the Raspberry festival nor the Cornhoeing. The Ripe Corn is celebrated at the Harvest Festival.

102. Festival of the Green Corn

When the Thanksgiving for the Green Corn comes, the special managers, both men and women, shall give it special attention and do their duties properly.

103. Ripe Corn Thanksgiving or Harvest Festival

When the Ripe Corn Thanksgiving is celebrated, the chiefs of the Nation must give it the same attention as they give to the Midwinter Thanksgiving.

104. About a good man

Whenever any man proves himself by his good life and his knowledge of good things, he shall be recognized by the chiefs as a Teacher of Peace and Kariwiio and the people shall hear him.

INSTALLATION SONG

105. Installation song by Atotarho

The song used on installing a new chief of the League shall be sung by Atotarho and it shall be:
"Haii, haii Akwa wiio   (It is good indeed
"Haii, haii Akonhewatha   That a broom,
"Haii, haii Skaweiesekowa   A great wing
"Haii, haii Yonkwawi   Is given me
"Haii, haii Iakonhewatha   For a sweeping instrument)

106. To learn the song of Peace

Whenever a person entitled properly desires to learn the Song of Peace, he is privileged to do so, but he must prepare a feast at which his teachers may sit with him and sing. The feast is provided that no misfortune may befall them for singing the song when no Chief is installed.

107. PROTECTION OF THE HOUSE

A certain sign shall be known to all the people of the Five Nations which shall denote that the owner or occupant of a house is absent. A stick or pole in a slanting or leaning position shall indicate this and be the sign. Every person not entitled to enter the house by right of living within upon seeing such a sign shall not enter the house by day or by night, but shall keep as far away as his business will permit.

Note: In these days of progress and enlightenment, such a sign would be an open invitation to burglars.

FUNERALS

108. At the funeral of a Chief

At the funeral of a chief of the League these words are said:

"Now we become reconciled as you start away. You were once a Chief of the League of Five Nations, and the united people trusted you. Now we release you for it is true that it is no longer possible for us to walk about together on the earth. Now therefore, we lay it (the body) here. Here we lay it away. Now then we say to you, persevere onward to the place where the Creator dwells in peace. Let not the things on the earth hinder you. Let nothing that transpired while you lived hinder you. In hunting, you once delighted; in the game of lacrosse, you once took delight, and in the feast and pleasant occasions your mind was amused, but now do not allow thoughts of these things to give you trouble.

"Let not your relatives hinder you and also let not your friends and associates trouble your mind. Regard none of these things.

"Now then, in turn, you here present who are related to the man, and you who were his friends and associates, behold the path that is yours also! Soon we ourselves will be left in that place. For this reason, hold yourselves in restraint as you go from place to place. In your actions and in your conversation do no idle thing. Speak not idle talk, neither gossip. Be careful of this and speak not and do not give away to evil behavior.

One year is the time that you must abstain from unseeming levity, but if you cannot do this for ceremony, ten days is the time to regard these things for respect."

109. At the funeral of a War Chief

At the funeral of a War Chief say:

Now we become reconciled as you start away. Once you were a War Chief of the Five Nations League and the United People trusted you as their guard from the enemy. (The remainder is the same as the address at the funeral of a chief.)

110. At the funeral of a warrior

At the funeral of a warrior, say:

Now we become reconciled as you start away. Once you were a devoted provider and protector of your family and you were ready to take part in battles for the Five Nations. The United People trusted you...(The remainder is the same as the address at the funeral of a chief.)

111. At the funeral of a young man

At the funeral of a young man, say:

Now we become reconciled as you start away. In the beginning of your career you are taken away and the flower of your life is withered away . . . (The remainder is the same as the address at the funeral of a chief.)

112. At the funeral of a Clan Mother

At the funeral of a Chief Women, say:

Now we become reconciled as you start away. You were once a Chief Woman in the League of Five Nations. You once were a Mother of the Nations. Now we release you for it is true that it is no longer possible for us to walk about together on the earth. Now, therefore, we lay it (the body) here. Here we lay it away. Now we say to you, persevere onward to the place where the Creator dwells in peace. Let not the things of the earth hinder you. Looking after your family was a sacred duty, and you were faithful. You were one of the joint heirs of the chieftainship titles. Feastings were yours and you had pleasant occasions . . . (The remainder of the address is the same as the address at the funeral of a chief.)

113. At the funeral of a young woman

At the funeral of a young woman, say:

Now we become reconciled as you start away. You were once a woman in the flower of life and the bloom is now withered away. You once held a sacred position as mother of the Nation... Looking after your family was a sacred duty and you were faithful. Feastings... (The remainder is the same as at the funeral of a chief.)

114. At the funeral of an infant or a young woman

At the funeral of an infant or young woman, say:

Now we become reconciled as you start away. You were a tender bud and gladdened our hearts for only a few days. Now the bloom has withered away... Let none of these things that transpired on earth hinder you. Let nothing that happened while you lived hinder you... (The remainder is as at the funeral of a chief.)

115. When an infant dies within three days

When an infant dies within three days, mourning shall continue only five days. Then shall you gather the little boys and girls at the house of mourning and at the funeral feast, a speaker shall address the children and bid them to be happy once more, though by death, gloom has been cast over them, then shall the children be again in the sunshine.

116. The Burial Rites

When a dead person is brought to the burial place, the speaker on the opposite side of the Council Fire shall bid the bereaved family to cheer up their minds once more and rekindle their fires in peace, to put their house in order and once again be in brightness for darkness has covered them. He shall say that the black clouds shall roll away and that the blue sky is visible once more. Therefore they shall be at peace in the sunshine again.

117. Speaking at the burial and at the tenth day of mourning

Three strings of shell one span in length shall be employed in addressing the assemblage at the burial of the dead. The speaker shall say:

"Hearken you who are here, this body is to be covered. Assemble in this place again in ten days hence, for it is the decree of the Creator that mourning shall cease when ten days have expired. Then a feast shall be made."

Then at the expiration of ten days, the Speaker shall say:

"Continue to listen you who are here. The ten days of mourning have expired and your mind must now be freed of sorrow as before the loss of your relative. The relatives have decided to make a little compensation to those who have assisted at the funeral. It is a mere expression of thanks. This is the one who did the cooking while the body was lying in the house. Let her come forward and receive this gift and be released from the task." (In substance, this will be repeated for everyone who assisted in any way until all have been remembered.)